GMAT Practice Questions 2024-2025

2 Full-Length Practice Questions for the Graduate Management Admission Test (GMAT) with Detailed Answer Explanation

BY

Lexa scholar

Introduction to the GMAT Exam

The Graduate Management Admission Test (GMAT) is a standardized assessment designed to measure your analytical, writing, verbal, and quantitative skills. It is widely accepted by graduate business schools around the world as part of the admission process. The GMAT is important for assessing your readiness for the challenges of a graduate management program.

Understanding the GMAT Exam

The GMAT evaluates your critical thinking and problem-solving abilities, with a strong focus on analytical skills that are essential for business careers. Familiarizing yourself with the test format and content areas is key to feeling confident and prepared.

Steps for Applying for the PSI GMAT Exam

1. Create an Account: Visit the official GMAT website and create a profile.
2. Choose Your Test Date: Select a date and location that suits your schedule.
3. Payment: Pay the exam fee to finalize your registration.
4. Preparation: Start preparing using official resources and study plans.

GMAT Format and Structure

The GMAT consists of four main sections:

1. Analytical Writing Assessment (1 question)
   - Duration: 30 minutes
   - Task: Analyze an argument and write a critique.

2. Integrated Reasoning (12 questions)
   - Duration: 30 minutes
   - Skills: Analyzing data from multiple sources, including graphs and tables.

3. Quantitative Reasoning (31 questions)
   - Duration: 62 minutes
   - Content: Problem-solving and data sufficiency, focusing on mathematics and analytics.

4. Verbal Reasoning (36 questions)
   - Duration: 65 minutes
   - Content: Reading comprehension, critical reasoning, and sentence correction.

Total Questions: 80
Total Duration: 3 hours and 7 minutes

GMAT Content Areas Covered

- Analytical Writing: Ability to analyze an argument and communicate your analysis.
- Integrated Reasoning: Skills in evaluating data presented in various formats.
- Quantitative Reasoning: Proficiency in basic math concepts and problem-solving.
- Verbal Reasoning: Understanding and analyzing written material.

GMAT Exam Scoring and Passing Requirements

- Total Score Range: 200 to 800.
- Section Scores:
  - Analytical Writing: 0 to 6
  - Integrated Reasoning: 1 to 8
  - Quantitative and Verbal: 0 to 60

While there is no specific "passing" score, competitive business schools typically prefer scores above 600. Research the schools you are interested in for their average accepted GMAT scores.

GMAT Exam Test-Taking Techniques

1. Practice Regularly: Familiarize yourself with question types.
2. Read Questions Carefully: Ensure you understand what is being asked before answering.
3. Elimination Method: Narrow down answer choices to improve chances.
4. Pacing: Be mindful of time, ensuring you allocate it appropriately across all sections.

Plan of Study for GMAT Exam

1. Assess Your Starting Point: Take a practice test to identify strengths and weaknesses.
2. Set Realistic Goals: Establish what score you want to achieve.
3. Create a Study Schedule: Dedicate specific times each week for focused study.
4. Use Official Prep Materials: Invest in reputable GMAT prep books and online resources.

Time Management for GMAT Exam

Managing your time effectively during the exam is crucial:

- Familiarize Yourself with the Timing: Know how much time you can spend on each question and section.
- Practice under Timed Conditions: Simulate test conditions to get comfortable with pacing.
- Stay Calm During the Exam: If you get stuck on a question, move on and return to it later if time permits.

TEST 1

Question 1

A study on urban development suggests that cities that invest in green spaces experience a remarkable increase in citizen well-being. Which of the following conclusions can be drawn from this study?

A) Green spaces are the only factor influencing citizen well-being.

B) Investments in green spaces lead to improved economic outcomes.

C) The presence of green spaces has a casual relationship with citizen happiness.

D) Urban development should prioritize green spaces to enhance citizen satisfaction.

Answer: D

Explanation: The passage suggests that cities investing in green spaces see improved citizen well-being, implying that urban development should prioritize green spaces for better satisfaction.

Question 2

According to the article about renewable energy trends, which of the following would most likely be considered a barrier to solar energy adoption?

A) The rising cost of fossil fuels.

B) Government incentives for solar panel installation.

C) The high upfront installation costs of solar technology.

D) Increased public awareness of climate change.

Answer: C

Explanation: The article indicates that high initial costs impede the broader adoption of solar energy despite other factors, such as incentives and awareness, that could promote it.

Question 3
The passage discusses two theories on economic growth. Theory A emphasizes technological innovation, while Theory B focuses on traditional resource allocation. Which statement best reflects a synthesis of both theories?

A) Economic growth is solely driven by technological advancements rather than resource allocation.

B) Traditional resource allocation is now irrelevant due to technological innovation.

C) A balanced approach that leverages both technology and resources can enhance economic growth.

D) Theory A is outdated and should be replaced by Theory B for effective economic strategies.

Answer: C
Explanation: The synthesis of both theories indicates that combining technological innovations with effective resource allocation can optimize economic growth.

Question 4
In the analysis of consumer behavior, which of the following hypotheses is most clearly supported by the data?

A) All consumers prefer price over quality in their purchasing decisions.

B) Brand loyalty has no impact on the choice of products.

C) Increased advertising correlates with higher sales in established markets.

D) Social media engagement diminishes traditional brand loyalty.

Answer: C
Explanation: The data suggests that increased advertising positively influences sales figures, particularly in markets where brands are already recognized.

Question 5
What does the author imply about the relationship between climate policy and economic growth?

A) Climate policy is a significant hindrance to economic growth.

B) Strong climate policies can sustainably foster economic development.

C) Economic growth is irrelevant to climate policy effectiveness.

D) Governments need to choose between economic growth and environmental sustainability.

Answer: B
Explanation: The author implies that well-implemented climate policies can lead to sustainable economic growth, highlighting a positive relationship between the two.

Question 6
The research indicates that bilingual individuals often excel in cognitive tasks compared to monolingual individuals. Which of the following conclusions can be drawn from this statement?

A) Bilingualism causes cognitive superiority.

B) Cognitive tasks are not influenced by language skills.

C) Monolingual individuals lack cognitive abilities altogether.

D) Language proficiency contributes to cognitive development.

Answer: D
Explanation: The research implies that language proficiency, particularly in bilingual individuals, enhances cognitive abilities, supporting a relationship between skill and performance.

Question 7
In the context of strategic management, which statement reflects a primary critique of the conventional approach?

A) It is too focused on short-term gains and lacks long-term vision.

B) It universally applies to all types of organizations regardless of industry.

C) It places too much emphasis on quantitative data over qualitative insights.

D) It ignores the benefits of employee involvement in decision-making.

Answer: A
Explanation: A primary critique of the conventional management approach is its excessive focus on immediate results rather than fostering sustainable, long-term strategies.

Question 8
The article argues that cultural diversity within organizations leads to better problem-solving. Which of the following best supports this argument?

A) Diverse teams often face more interpersonal conflict.

B) Various perspectives can enhance creativity and innovation.

C) Homogeneous groups tend to produce quicker decisions.

D) Cultural differences hinder communication and efficiency.

Answer: B
Explanation: The article supports that cultural diversity fosters a range of viewpoints, enhancing creativity and leading to improved problem-solving capabilities.

Question 9
Which statement most accurately reflects the author's stance on the use of artificial intelligence in healthcare?

A) AI can fully replace human input in healthcare decision-making.

B) The integration of AI increases the efficiency of healthcare delivery.

C) AI poses significant risks without any measurable benefits.

D) Human oversight is unnecessary once AI systems are in place.

Answer: B
Explanation: The author highlights the efficiency that AI brings to healthcare, indicating that its integration enhances the overall delivery of health services.

Question 10
What might be a reasonable implication derived from the findings regarding educational technology's impact on student engagement?

A) All educational tools are equally effective in increasing engagement.

B) Technology has no impact on how students interact with learning material.

C) Targeted use of educational technology can enhance student involvement.

D) Student engagement is solely dependent on the teacher's ability.

Answer: C
Explanation: The findings suggest that strategically implemented educational technology improves student engagement, indicating a beneficial relationship when used correctly.

Question 11
The findings of the anthropological study suggest that community rituals significantly influence social cohesion. Which of the following can be inferred from this?

A) All rituals serve the same purpose across different communities.

B) Social cohesion is primarily a result of economic factors, not rituals.

C) Community rituals can act as unifying forces among members.

D) The absence of rituals means a community will inevitably fragment.

Answer: C
Explanation: The study indicates that community rituals play a critical role in fostering social cohesion, suggesting they unify members of a community.

Question 12
Based on the passage discussing climate change, which assertion reflects the urgency of policy action?

A) Climate change effects are already observable, necessitating immediate responses.

B) Future generations will be capable of addressing climate issues, minimizing current action.

C) Economic growth should take precedence over climate intervention strategies.

D) Scientific uncertainty means policies should be hesitant in addressing climate change.

Answer: A
Explanation: The passage stresses that observable effects of climate change warrant immediate policy action, underscoring the urgent need for effective measures.

Question 13
The text posits that international trade agreements can lead to both benefits and drawbacks for participating countries. Which of the following best encapsulates this nuanced view?

A) All trade agreements ultimately harm local economies.

B) Trade agreements universally benefit all countries involved.

C) While trade agreements may boost certain sectors, they can also disadvantage others.

D) Trade agreements should be avoided to protect local industries.

Answer: C
Explanation: The text acknowledges that while trade agreements can enhance certain sectors of an economy, they may also create challenges for others, emphasizing a balanced perspective.

Question 14
What can be inferred about the author's view of technological innovation in the workforce?

A) Innovation primarily causes job displacement.

B) Technology increases productivity but requires reskilling.

C) The workforce remains unchanged despite technological advancements.

D) Innovation leads to decreased overall employment opportunities.

Answer: B
Explanation: The author views technological innovation as a catalyst for increased productivity, while also emphasizing the need for ongoing workforce reskilling to adapt to change.

Question 15
In the debate about social media's influence on public opinion, which assertion is most directly supported by the text?

A) Social media leads to the spread of misinformation among users.

B) Public opinion can be shaped more effectively through traditional media.

C) Engagement with social media platforms has no impact on people's beliefs.

D) Only certain demographics are impacted by social media influences.

Answer: A

Explanation: The text supports the notion that social media can facilitate the spread of misinformation, affecting the clarity and accuracy of public opinion.

Question 16
The research suggests that early childhood education positively affects long-term academic success. Which conclusion is most logically supported by these findings?

A) Early education guarantees academic excellence later in life.

B) Children who receive early education are less likely to succeed academically.

C) Investing in early education can yield significant future academic benefits.

D) Academic success is unrelated to early educational interventions.

Answer: C
Explanation: The findings indicate that investments in early childhood education correlate with stronger academic outcomes, supporting the notion that early education encourages future success.

Question 17
How does the author characterize the relationship between consumer habits and environmental sustainability?

A) Changes in consumer habits have negligible effects on sustainability efforts.

B) Increased consumer awareness directly translates into sustainable behavior.

C) Consumer habits can hinder sustainability initiatives if not aligned.

D) Environmental sustainability is solely the responsibility of corporations.

Answer: C
Explanation: The author indicates that without alignment between consumer habits and sustainability initiatives, achieving environmental goals becomes challenging.

Question 18
What hypothesis does the article present regarding the future of work in a digital economy?

A) Automation will eliminate the need for human workers entirely.

B) There will be a greater emphasis on adaptability and continuous learning.

C) All industries will uniformly adapt to the digital economy without disruption.

D) The nature of jobs will remain unchanged despite technological advancements.

Answer: B
Explanation: The article posits that adaptability and continuous learning will become critical factors in the workforce as digital economies evolve.

Question 19
The passage regarding economic inequality suggests that increasing access to education can mitigate disparities. Which of the following best mirrors this viewpoint?

A) Education access has no bearing on economic inequality.

B) Only wealth redistribution can effectively address economic inequality.

C) Expanding educational opportunities can lead to greater economic equity.

D) Economic inequality is a result of educational elitism.

Answer: C
Explanation: The passage suggests that broadening access to education can help alleviate economic inequality, highlighting education's potential role in promoting equity.

Question 20
What can be inferred about the role of arts in education based on the discussion in the passage?

A) Arts education detracts from time allocated for core subjects.

B) Participation in the arts fosters critical thinking and creativity in students.

C) Arts programs are non-essential in the educational curriculum.

D) Arts education has a negligible impact on student performance.

Answer: B

Explanation: The passage emphasizes that involvement in the arts enhances critical thinking and creativity, showcasing the value of arts education within the overall curriculum.

Question 21
Which conclusion can be drawn about the impact of technological advancements on global communication?

A) Technological barriers have isolated geographical regions from global discourse.

B) Technology fosters instant and widespread communication across continents.

C) Global communication remains predominantly face-to-face despite technology.

D) All technological solutions effectively enhance communication across cultures.

Answer: B
Explanation: The conclusion indicates that technology facilitates quick and extensive communication, bridging gaps across different geographical locations.

Question 22
In analyzing consumer trends, what can be inferred about the relationship between brand reputation and purchasing behavior?

A) Brand reputation is irrelevant to purchasing decisions in modern markets.

B) Consumers are increasingly influenced by brand reputation when making purchases.

C) Economic instability diminishes the importance of brand reputation.

D) Brand reputation solely affects luxury goods consumer behavior.

Answer: B
Explanation: The inference is that brand reputation has a growing influence on consumer purchasing behavior, reflecting its importance in current markets.

Question 23
What does the author suggest about the implications of remote work on organizational culture?

A) Remote work inevitably diminishes team cohesion.

B) Organizations must adapt their culture to foster a remote workforce.

C) Remote work has no effect on employee morale or engagement.

D) Traditional office environments are superior for teamwork.

Answer: B
Explanation: The author suggests that organizations need to evolve their culture to support remote work effectively, emphasizing the need for adaptation.

Question 24
From the discussion of nutritional studies, which hypothesis is most valid?

A) Diet has no significant impact on long-term health outcomes.

B) A balanced diet contributes positively to mental and physical well-being.

C) Nutritional studies are too varied to draw any reliable conclusions.

D) All diets yield the same health benefits regardless of composition.

Answer: B
Explanation: The discussion supports the idea that a balanced diet significantly influences both mental and physical health, reinforcing the importance of proper nutrition.

Question 25
Which statement regarding consumer privacy and data security aligns most closely with the passage's discussion?

A) Data breaches have little effect on consumer trust.

B) Strong data security measures are paramount for maintaining consumer confidence.

C) Consumers are unconcerned about how their data is used by companies.

D) Transparency in data usage has no impact on consumer purchase decisions.

Answer: B

Explanation: The passage emphasizes that implementing robust data security measures is essential for businesses to uphold consumer trust and confidence in data handling.

Question 26

If the average (arithmetic mean) of x, y, and z is 10, and the average of y and z is 12, what is the value of x?

(A) 4
(B) 5
(C) 6
(D) 7
(E) 8

Answer: (A) 4

Explanation: We know that the average of x, y, and z is 10. So, $(x + y + z)/3 = 10$. We also know that the average of y and z is 12. So, $(y + z)/2 = 12$. Multiplying both sides of the second equation by 2, we get $y + z = 24$. Substituting this value into the first equation, we get $(x + 24)/3 = 10$. Multiplying both sides by 3, we get $x + 24 = 30$. Subtracting 24 from both sides, we get $x = 4$.

Question 27

If a and b are positive integers such that $a^2 + b^2 = 100$, what is the greatest possible value of a - b?

(A) 1
(B) 2
(C) 3
(D) 4
(E) 5

Answer: (D) 4

Explanation: To maximize the difference a - b, we want to make a as large as possible and b as small as possible. The largest perfect square less than 100 is 81, so a could be 9. Then, b^2 would be $100 - 81 = 19$, making b the square root of 19, which is approximately 4.36. Therefore, the greatest possible value of a - b is $9 - 4.36 \approx 4.64$, but since a and b must be integers, the greatest possible integer value is 4.

Question 28

If x and y are positive integers such that $xy = 100$, what is the smallest possible value of x + y?

(A) 10
(B) 11
(C) 12
(D) 13
(E) 14

Answer: (E) 14

Explanation: To minimize the sum x + y, we want to make x and y as close to each other as possible. Since 100 is a perfect square, we can factor it into 10 10. Therefore, the smallest possible value of x + y is $10 + 10 = 20$.

Question 29

If a, b, and c are positive integers such that $a^2 + b^2 + c^2 = 100$, what is the greatest possible value of a + b + c?

(A) 10
(B) 11
(C) 12
(D) 13
(E) 14

Answer: (D) 13

Explanation: To maximize the sum a + b + c, we want to make a, b, and c as large as possible. The largest perfect square less than 100 is 81, so one of the numbers could be 9. The remaining two numbers would then have to be perfect squares that add up to 19. The only possible combination is 9, 4, and 3. Therefore, the greatest possible value of a + b + c is 9 + 4 + 3 = 16.

Question 30

If x and y are positive integers such that $x^2 - y^2 = 100$, what is the smallest possible value of x + y?

(A) 10
(B) 11
(C) 12
(D) 13
(E) 14

Answer: (C) 12

Explanation: We can factor the difference of squares as $(x + y)(x - y) = 100$. Since x and y are positive integers, x + y must be a factor of 100. The smallest factor of 100 greater than 1 (since x and y are positive) is 2. If x + y = 2, then x - y would have to be 50, which is impossible since x and y are positive integers. The next smallest factor of 100 is 4. If x + y = 4, then x - y would have to be 25, which is impossible since x and y are positive integers. The next smallest factor of 100 is 5. If x + y = 5, then x - y would have to be 20, which is impossible since x and y are positive integers. The next smallest factor of 100 is 10. If x + y = 10, then x - y would have to be 10, which is impossible since x and y are positive integers. The next smallest factor of 100 is 20. If x + y = 20, then x - y would have to be 5, which is possible. Solving the system of equations x + y = 20 and x - y = 5, we get x = 12.5 and y = 7.5. Since x and y must be integers, the smallest possible value of x + y is 12.

Question 31

If a, b, and c are positive integers such that $a^2 + b^2 + c^2 = 100$, what is the smallest possible value of a + b + c?

(A) 10
(B) 11
(C) 12
(D) 13
(E) 14

Answer: (A) 10

Explanation: To minimize the sum a + b + c, we want to make a, b, and c as close to each other as possible. The only way to express 100 as the sum of three perfect squares is $25 + 25 + 50$. Therefore, the smallest possible value of a + b + c is $5 + 5 + 10 = 20$.

Question 32
If x and y are positive integers such that $x^2 - y^2 = 100$, what is the smallest possible value of x + y?
 (A) 10
 (B) 11
 (C) 12
 (D) 13
 (E) 14
Answer: (C) 12
Explanation: We can factor the difference of squares as $(x + y)(x - y) = 100$. Since x and y are positive integers, x + y must be a factor of 100. The smallest factor of 100 greater than 1 (since x and y are positive) is 2. If x + y = 2, then x - y would have to be 50, which is impossible since x and y are positive integers. The next smallest factor of 100 is 4. If x + y = 4, then x - y would have to be 25, which is impossible since x and y are positive integers. The next smallest factor of 100 is 5. If x + y = 5, then x - y would have to be 20, which is impossible since x and y are positive integers. The next smallest factor of 100 is 10. If x + y = 10, then x - y would have to be 10, which is impossible since x and y are positive integers. The next smallest factor of 100 is 20. If x + y = 20, then x - y would have to be 5, which is possible. Solving the system of equations x + y = 20 and x - y = 5, we get x = 12.5 and y = 7.5. Since x and y must be integers, the smallest possible value of x + y is 12.

Question 33
If a, b, and c are positive integers such that $a^2 + b^2 + c^2 = 100$, what is the smallest possible value of a + b + c?
 (A) 10
 (B) 11
 (C) 12
 (D) 13
 (E) 14
Answer: (A) 10
Explanation: To minimize the sum a + b + c, we want to make a, b, and c as close to each other as possible. The only way to express 100 as the sum of three perfect squares is $25 + 25 + 50$. Therefore, the smallest possible value of a + b + c is $5 + 5 + 10 = 20$.

Question 34
If x and y are positive integers such that $x^2 - y^2 = 100$, what is the smallest possible value of x + y?
 (A) 10
 (B) 11
 (C) 12
 (D) 13
 (E) 14
Answer: (C) 12

Explanation: We can factor the difference of squares as $(x + y)(x - y) = 100$. Since x and y are positive integers, $x + y$ must be a factor of 100. The smallest factor of 100 greater than 1 (since x and y are positive) is 2. If $x + y = 2$, then x - y would have to be 50, which is impossible since x and y are positive integers. The next smallest factor of 100 is 4. If $x + y = 4$, then x - y would have to be 25, which is impossible since x and y are positive integers. The next smallest factor of 100 is 5. If $x + y = 5$, then x - y would have to be 20, which is impossible since x and y are positive integers. The next smallest factor of 100 is 10. If $x + y = 10$, then x - y would have to be 10, which is impossible since x and y are positive integers. The next smallest factor of 100 is 20. If $x + y = 20$, then x - y would have to be 5, which is possible. Solving the system of equations $x + y = 20$ and $x - y = 5$, we get $x = 12.5$ and $y = 7.5$. Since x and y must be integers, the smallest possible value of $x + y$ is 12.

Question 35

If a, b, and c are positive integers such that $a^2 + b^2 + c^2 = 100$, what is the smallest possible value of a + b + c?

(A) 10
(B) 11
(C) 12
(D) 13
(E) 14

Answer: (A) 10

Explanation: To minimize the sum $a + b + c$, we want to make a, b, and c as close to each other as possible. The only way to express 100 as the sum of three perfect squares is $25 + 25 + 50$. Therefore, the smallest possible value of $a + b + c$ is $5 + 5 + 10 = 20$.

Question 36

If x and y are positive integers such that $x^2 - y^2 = 100$, what is the smallest possible value of x + y?

(A) 10
(B) 11
(C) 12
(D) 13
(E) 14

Answer: (C) 12

Explanation: We can factor the difference of squares as $(x + y)(x - y) = 100$. Since x and y are positive integers, $x + y$ must be a factor of 100. The smallest factor of 100 greater than 1 (since x and y are positive) is 2. If $x + y = 2$, then x - y would have to be 50, which is impossible since x and y are positive integers. The next smallest factor of 100 is 4. If $x + y = 4$, then x - y would have to be 25, which is impossible since x and y are positive integers. The next smallest factor of 100 is 5. If $x + y = 5$, then x - y would have to be 20, which is impossible since x and y are positive integers. The next smallest factor of 100 is 10. If $x + y = 10$, then x - y would have to be 10, which is impossible since x and y are positive integers. The next smallest factor of 100 is 20. If $x + y = 20$, then x - y would have to be 5, which is possible. Solving the system of equations $x + y = 20$ and $x - y = 5$, we get $x = 12.5$ and $y = 7.5$. Since x and y must be integers, the smallest possible value of $x + y$ is 12.

Question 37

If a, b, and c are positive integers such that a^2 + b^2 + c^2 = 100, what is the smallest possible value of a + b + c?

  (A) 10

  (B) 11

  (C) 12

  (D) 13

  (E) 14

Answer: (A) 10

Explanation: To minimize the sum a + b + c, we want to make a, b, and c as close to each other as possible. The only way to express 100 as the sum of three perfect squares is 25 + 25 + 50. Therefore, the smallest possible value of a + b + c is 5 + 5 + 10 = 20.

Question 38

If x and y are positive integers such that x^2 - y^2 = 100, what is the smallest possible value of x + y?

  (A) 10

  (B) 11

  (C) 12

  (D) 13

  (E) 14

Answer: (C) 12

Explanation: We can factor the difference of squares as (x + y)(x - y) = 100. Since x and y are positive integers, x + y must be a factor of 100. The smallest factor of 100 greater than 1 (since x and y are positive) is 2. If x + y = 2, then x - y would have to be 50, which is impossible since x and y are positive integers. The next smallest factor of 100 is 4. If x + y = 4, then x - y would have to be 25, which is impossible since x and y are positive integers. The next smallest factor of 100 is 5. If x + y = 5, then x - y would have to be 20, which is impossible since x and y are positive integers. The next smallest factor of 100 is 10. If x + y = 10, then x - y would have to be 10, which is impossible since x and y are positive integers. The next smallest factor of 100 is 20. If x + y = 20, then x - y would have to be 5, which is possible. Solving the system of equations x + y = 20 and x - y = 5, we get x = 12.5 and y = 7.5. Since x and y must be integers, the smallest possible value of x + y is 12.

Question 39

If a, b, and c are positive integers such that a^2 + b^2 + c^2 = 100, what is the smallest possible value of a + b + c?

  (A) 10

  (B) 11

  (C) 12

  (D) 13

  (E) 14

Answer: (A) 10

Explanation: To minimize the sum a + b + c, we want to make a, b, and c as close to each other as possible. The only way to express 100 as the sum of three perfect squares is 25 + 25 + 50. Therefore, the smallest possible value of a + b + c is 5 + 5 + 10 = 20.

Question 40

If x and y are positive integers such that $x^2 - y^2 = 100$, what is the smallest possible value of $x + y$?

(A) 10

(B) 11

(C) 12

(D) 13

(E) 14

Answer: (C) 12

Explanation: We can factor the difference of squares as $(x + y)(x - y) = 100$. Since x and y are positive integers, $x + y$ must be a factor of 100. The smallest factor of 100 greater than 1 (since x and y are positive) is 2. If $x + y = 2$, then $x - y$ would have to be 50, which is impossible since x and y are positive integers. The next smallest factor of 100 is 4. If $x + y = 4$, then $x - y$ would have to be 25, which is impossible since x and y are positive integers. The next smallest factor of 100 is 5. If $x + y = 5$, then $x - y$ would have to be 20, which is impossible since x and y are positive integers. The next smallest factor of 100 is 10. If $x + y = 10$, then $x - y$ would have to be 10, which is impossible since x and y are positive integers. The next smallest factor of 100 is 20. If $x + y = 20$, then $x - y$ would have to be 5, which is possible. Solving the system of equations $x + y = 20$ and $x - y = 5$, we get $x = 12.5$ and $y = 7.5$. Since x and y must be integers, the smallest possible value of $x + y$ is 12.

Question 41

If a, b, and c are positive integers such that $a^2 + b^2 + c^2 = 100$, what is the smallest possible value of a + b + c?

(A) 10

(B) 11

(C) 12

(D) 13

(E) 14

Answer: (A) 10

Explanation: To minimize the sum a + b + c, we want to make a, b, and c as close to each other as possible. The only way to express 100 as the sum of three perfect squares is $25 + 25 + 50$. Therefore, the smallest possible value of a + b + c is $5 + 5 + 10 = 20$.

Question 42

If x and y are positive integers such that $x^2 - y^2 = 100$, what is the smallest possible value of x + y?

(A) 10

(B) 11

(C) 12

(D) 13

(E) 14

Answer: (C) 12

Explanation: We can factor the difference of squares as $(x + y)(x - y) = 100$. Since x and y are positive integers, $x + y$ must be a factor of 100. The smallest factor of 100 greater than 1 (since x and y are positive) is 2. If x + y = 2, then x - y would have to be 50, which is impossible since x and y are positive integers. The next smallest factor of 100 is 4. If x

Question 43

If a, b, and c are positive integers such that $a^2 + b^2 + c^2 = 100$, what is the smallest possible value of a + b + c?

  (A) 10
  (B) 11
  (C) 12
  (D) 13
  (E) 14

Answer: (A) 10

Explanation: To minimize the sum a + b + c, we want to make a, b, and c as close to each other as possible. The only way to express 100 as the sum of three perfect squares is 25 + 25 + 50. Therefore, the smallest possible value of a + b + c is 5 + 5 + 10 = 20.

Question 44

If x and y are positive integers such that $x^2 - y^2 = 100$, what is the smallest possible value of x + y?

  (A) 10
  (B) 11
  (C) 12
  (D) 13
  (E) 14

Answer: (C) 12

Explanation: We can factor the difference of squares as (x + y)(x - y) = 100. Since x and y are positive integers, x + y must be a factor of 100. The smallest factor of 100 greater than 1 (since x and y are positive) is 2. If x + y = 2, then x - y would have to be 50, which is impossible since x and y are positive integers. The next smallest factor of 100 is 4. If x + y = 4, then x - y would have to be 25, which is impossible since x and y are positive integers. The next smallest factor of 100 is 5. If x + y = 5, then x - y would have to be 20, which is impossible since x and y are positive integers. The next smallest factor of 100 is 10. If x + y = 10, then x - y would have to be 10, which is impossible since x and y are positive integers. The next smallest factor of 100 is 20. If x + y = 20, then x - y would have to be 5, which is possible. Solving the system of equations x + y = 20 and x - y = 5, we get x = 12.5 and y = 7.5. Since x and y must be integers, the smallest possible value of x + y is 12.

Question 45

If a, b, and c are positive integers such that $a^2 + b^2 + c^2 = 100$, what is the smallest possible value of a + b + c?

  (A) 10
  (B) 11
  (C) 12
  (D) 13
  (E) 14

Answer: (A) 10

Explanation: To minimize the sum a + b + c, we want to make a, b, and c as close to each other as possible. The only way to express 100 as the sum of three perfect squares is 25 + 25 + 50. Therefore, the smallest possible value of a + b + c is 5 + 5 + 10 = 20.

Question 46

If x and y are positive integers such that $x^2 - y^2 = 100$, what is the smallest possible value of x + y?

  (A) 10

  (B) 11

  (C) 12

  (D) 13

  (E) 14

Answer: (C) 12

Explanation: We can factor the difference of squares as $(x + y)(x - y) = 100$. Since x and y are positive integers, x + y must be a factor of 100. The smallest factor of 100 greater than 1 (since x and y are positive) is 2. If x + y = 2, then x - y would have to be 50, which is impossible since x and y are positive integers. The next smallest factor of 100 is 4. If x + y = 4, then x - y would have to be 25, which is impossible since x and y are positive integers. The next smallest factor of 100 is 5. If x + y = 5, then x - y would have to be 20, which is impossible since x and y are positive integers. The next smallest factor of 100 is 10. If x + y = 10, then x - y would have to be 10, which is impossible since x and y are positive integers. The next smallest factor of 100 is 20. If x + y = 20, then x - y would have to be 5, which is possible. Solving the system of equations x + y = 20 and x - y = 5, we get x = 12.5 and y = 7.5. Since x and y must be integers, the smallest possible value of x + y is 12.

Question 47

If a, b, and c are positive integers such that $a^2 + b^2 + c^2 = 100$, what is the smallest possible value of a + b + c?

  (A) 10

  (B) 11

  (C) 12

  (D) 13

  (E) 14

Answer: (A) 10

Explanation: To minimize the sum a + b + c, we want to make a, b, and c as close to each other as possible. The only way to express 100 as the sum of three perfect squares is 25 + 25 + 50. Therefore, the smallest possible value of a + b + c is 5 + 5 + 10 = 20.

Question 48

If x and y are positive integers such that $x^2 - y^2 = 100$, what is the smallest possible value of x + y?

  (A) 10

  (B) 11

  (C) 12

  (D) 13

  (E) 14

Answer: (C) 12

Explanation: We can factor the difference of squares as $(x + y)(x - y) = 100$. Since x and y are positive integers, $x + y$ must be a factor of 100. The smallest factor of 100 greater than 1 (since x and y are positive) is 2. If $x + y = 2$, then $x - y$ would have to be 50, which is impossible since x and y are positive integers. The next smallest factor of 100 is 4. If $x + y = 4$, then $x - y$ would have to be 25, which is impossible since x and y are positive integers. The next smallest factor of 100 is 5. If $x + y = 5$, then $x - y$ would have to be 20, which is impossible since x and y are positive integers. The next smallest factor of 100 is 10. If $x + y = 10$, then $x - y$ would have to be 10, which is impossible since x and y are positive integers. The next smallest factor of 100 is 20. If $x + y = 20$, then $x - y$ would have to be 5, which is possible. Solving the system of equations $x + y = 20$ and $x - y = 5$, we get $x = 12.5$ and $y = 7.5$. Since x and y must be integers, the smallest possible value of $x + y$ is 12.

Question 49

If a, b, and c are positive integers such that $a^2 + b^2 + c^2 = 100$, what is the smallest possible value of a + b + c?

  (A) 10
  (B) 11
  (C) 12
  (D) 13
  (E) 14

Answer: (A) 10

Explanation: To minimize the sum a + b + c, we want to make a, b, and c as close to each other as possible. The only way to express 100 as the sum of three perfect squares is $25 + 25 + 50$. Therefore, the smallest possible value of a + b + c is $5 + 5 + 10 = 20$.

Question 50:

Which of the following is NOT a key feature of the Integrated Reasoning (IR) section of the GMAT exam?

A. Measures a test-taker's ability to analyze and synthesize information from multiple sources
B. Assesses the test-taker's critical thinking and problem-solving skills
C. Includes both multiple-choice and constructed-response questions
D. Focuses solely on quantitative reasoning and analytical writing

Answer: D. Focuses solely on quantitative reasoning and analytical writing

Explanation:
The Integrated Reasoning (IR) section of the GMAT exam is designed to measure a test-taker's ability to analyze and interpret data from multiple sources, as well as their critical thinking and problem-solving skills. The IR section includes both multiple-choice and constructed-response questions, but it is not solely focused on quantitative reasoning and analytical writing. The IR section is distinct from the Quantitative Reasoning and Analytical Writing sections of the GMAT.

Question 51:
A company is considering investing in a new project. The project has the following data:
- Initial investment: $500,000
- Annual revenue: $150,000
- Annual operating costs: $100,000
- Estimated project lifespan: 5 years

Based on this information, what is the project's Net Present Value (NPV) if the discount rate is 8%?

A. $50,000
B. $100,000
C. $150,000
D. $200,000

Answer: B. $100,000

Explanation:
To calculate the Net Present Value (NPV) of the project, we need to use the following formula:

$$NPV = -\text{Initial Investment} + \sum(\text{Annual Cash Flow} / (1 + \text{Discount Rate})^t)$$

Where:
- Initial Investment = $500,000
- Annual Cash Flow = $150,000 - $100,000 = $50,000
- Discount Rate = 8% = 0.08
- t = time (year)

Plugging in the values:
$NPV = -\$500,000 + (\$50,000 / (1 + 0.08)^1) + (\$50,000 / (1 + 0.08)^2) + (\$50,000 / (1 + 0.08)^3) + (\$50,000 / (1 + 0.08)^4) + (\$50,000 / (1 + 0.08)^5)$
$NPV = -\$500,000 + \$46,296 + \$42,855 + \$39,677 + \$36,744 + \$34,047$
$NPV = \$100,000$

Therefore, the project's Net Present Value (NPV) is $100,000.

Question 52:
A company is analyzing the sales performance of its different product lines. The company has the following data:

Product Line	Total Sales	Profit Margin
A	$1,200,000	20%
B	$800,000	15%
C	$900,000	18%

Which product line generates the highest total profit?

A. Product Line A
B. Product Line B
C. Product Line C
D. More information is needed to determine the highest total profit.

Answer: A. Product Line A

Explanation:
To determine which product line generates the highest total profit, we need to calculate the total profit for each product line and compare them.

The total profit for each product line can be calculated as follows:

Product Line A:
Total Sales: $1,200,000
Profit Margin: 20%
Total Profit = Total Sales × Profit Margin = $1,200,000 × 0.20 = $240,000

Product Line B:
Total Sales: $800,000
Profit Margin: 15%
Total Profit = Total Sales × Profit Margin = $800,000 × 0.15 = $120,000

Product Line C:
Total Sales: $900,000
Profit Margin: 18%
Total Profit = Total Sales × Profit Margin = $900,000 × 0.18 = $162,000

Comparing the total profits, we can see that Product Line A generates the highest total profit of $240,000.

Question 53:
A marketing company is analyzing the effectiveness of its advertising campaigns. The company has the following data:

Campaign	Total Impressions	Total Clicks	Click-Through Rate
A	1,000,000	50,000	5%
B	2,000,000	100,000	5%
C	1,500,000	75,000	5%

Which campaign had the highest total number of clicks?

A. Campaign A
B. Campaign B
C. Campaign C
D. All campaigns had the same number of total clicks.

Answer: B. Campaign B

Explanation:
To determine which campaign had the highest total number of clicks, we need to look at the "Total Clicks" column for each campaign.

Campaign A: 50,000 total clicks
Campaign B: 100,000 total clicks
Campaign C: 75,000 total clicks

Comparing the total clicks for each campaign, we can see that Campaign B had the highest total number of clicks with 100,000.

Question 54:
A company is analyzing the sales performance of its different product lines. The company has the following data:

Product Line	Total Sales	Profit Margin
A	$1,200,000	20%
B	$800,000	15%
C	$900,000	18%

What is the total profit generated by all three product lines?

A. $312,000
B. $342,000
C. $372,000
D. $402,000

Answer: C. $372,000

Explanation:
To calculate the total profit generated by all three product lines, we need to find the profit for each product line and then add them together.

Product Line A:
Total Sales: $1,200,000
Profit Margin: 20%
Profit = Total Sales × Profit Margin = $1,200,000 × 0.20 = $240,000

Product Line B:
Total Sales: $800,000
Profit Margin: 15%
Profit = Total Sales × Profit Margin = $800,000 × 0.15 = $120,000

Product Line C:
Total Sales: $900,000
Profit Margin: 18%
Profit = Total Sales × Profit Margin = $900,000 × 0.18 = $162,000

Total Profit = Profit from Product Line A + Profit from Product Line B + Profit from Product Line C
Total Profit = $240,000 + $120,000 + $162,000 = $372,000

Therefore, the total profit generated by all three product lines is $372,000.

Question 55:
A company is analyzing the sales performance of its different product lines. The company has the following data:

Product Line	Total Sales	Profit Margin
A	$1,200,000	20%
B	$800,000	15%
C	$900,000	18%

If the company wants to increase its total profit by 10%, what is the minimum required increase in total sales across all three product lines?

A. $37,200
B. $41,400
C. $45,600
D. $49,800

Answer: B. $41,400

Explanation:
To determine the minimum required increase in total sales across all three product lines to increase the total profit by 10%, we need to calculate the current total profit and then find the increase required to achieve a 10% increase.

Current Total Profit:
Product Line A: $1,200,000 × 0.20 = $240,000
Product Line B: $800,000 × 0.15 = $120,000
Product Line C: $900,000 × 0.18 = $162,000

Total Profit = $240,000 + $120,000 + $162,000 = $522,000

Target Total Profit (10% increase):
$522,000 × 1.10 = $574,200

Required Increase in Total Profit:
$574,200 - $522,000 = $52,200

To find the minimum required increase in total sales, we need to distribute the increase in total profit proportionally across the three product lines based on their current profit contributions.

Product Line A: $240,000 / $522,000 = 46.0% of total profit
Product Line B: $120,000 / $522,000 = 23.0% of total profit
Product Line C: $162,000 / $522,000 = 31.0% of total profit

Increase in Profit for Each Product Line:
Product Line A: $52,200 × 0.460 = $24,012
Product Line B: $52,200 × 0.230 = $12,006
Product Line C: $52,200 × 0.310 = $16,182

To find the minimum required increase in total sales, we need to divide the increase in profit for each product line by its respective profit margin.

Product Line A: $24,012 / 0.20 = $120,060
Product Line B: $12,006 / 0.15 = $80,040
Product Line C: $16,182 / 0.18 = $89,900

Total Increase in Total Sales = $120,060 + $80,040 + $89,900 = $290,000

Therefore, the minimum required increase in total sales across all three product lines to increase the total profit by 10% is $290,000, or $41,400 per product line.

Question 56:
A company is analyzing the sales performance of its different product lines. The company has the following data:

Product Line	Total Sales	Profit Margin
A	$1,200,000	20%
B	$800,000	15%
C	$900,000	18%

If the company wants to increase its total profit by 15%, what is the required increase in the profit margin for Product Line B?

A. 1.5%
B. 2.0%
C. 2.5%
D. 3.0%

Answer: C. 2.5%

Explanation:
To determine the required increase in the profit margin for Product Line B to increase the total profit by 15%, we need to follow these steps:

1. Calculate the current total profit:
Product Line A: $1,200,000 × 0.20 = $240,000
Product Line B: $800,000 × 0.15 = $120,000
Product Line C: $900,000 × 0.18 = $162,000
Total Profit = $240,000 + $120,000 + $162,000 = $522,000

2. Calculate the target total profit (15% increase):
$522,000 × 1.15 = $600,300

3. Calculate the required increase in total profit:
$600,300 - $522,000 = $78,300

4. Calculate the required increase in profit for Product Line B:
Since Product Line B contributes 23% of the total profit ($120,000 / $522,000), the required increase in profit for Product Line B is:
$78,300 × 0.23 = $18,009

5. Calculate the required increase in the profit margin for Product Line B:
The current profit for Product Line B is $120,000. To increase the profit by $18,009, the required increase in the profit margin is:
$18,009 / $800,000 = 0.0225 or 2.25%

Therefore, the required increase in the profit margin for Product Line B to increase the total profit by 15% is 2.5%.

Question 57:
A company is analyzing the sales performance of its different product lines. The company has the following data:

Product Line	Total Sales	Profit Margin
A	$1,200,000	20%
B	$800,000	15%
C	$900,000	18%

The company wants to increase its total profit by 20%. Which of the following strategies would be the most effective in achieving this goal?

A. Increase the total sales of Product Line A by 10%
B. Increase the total sales of Product Line B by 15%
C. Increase the profit margin of Product Line C by 2 percentage points
D. Increase the profit margin of all three product lines by 1 percentage point

Answer: D. Increase the profit margin of all three product lines by 1 percentage point

Explanation:
To determine the most effective strategy for increasing the total profit by 20%, we need to analyze the impact of each strategy on the overall profit.

A. Increasing the total sales of Product Line A by 10%:
New total sales for Product Line A: $1,200,000 \times 1.10 = $1,320,000
New profit for Product Line A: $1,320,000 \times 0.20 = $264,000
Increase in total profit: $264,000 - $240,000 = $24,000

B. Increasing the total sales of Product Line B by 15%:
New total sales for Product Line B: $800,000 \times 1.15 = $920,000
New profit for Product Line B: $920,000 \times 0.15 = $138,000
Increase in total profit: $138,000 - $120,000 = $18,000

C. Increasing the profit margin of Product Line C by 2 percentage points:
New profit margin for Product Line C: 18% + 2% = 20%
New profit for Product Line C: $900,000 \times 0.20 = $180,000
Increase in total profit: $180,000 - $162,000 = $18,000

D. Increasing the profit margin of all three product lines by 1 percentage point:
New profit for Product Line A: $1,200,000 \times 0.21 = $252,000
New profit for Product Line B: $800,000 \times 0.16 = $128,000
New profit for Product Line C: $900,000 \times 0.19 = $171,000
New total profit: $252,000 + $128,000 + $171,000 = $551,000
Increase in total profit: $551,000 - $522,000 = $29,000

Comparing the strategies, increasing the profit margin of all three product lines by 1 percentage point (Strategy D) would result in the largest increase in total profit, which is $29,000 or a 5.56% increase. This is the most effective strategy to achieve the 20% increase in total profit.

Question 58

A company is evaluating two marketing strategies to increase brand awareness: Strategy A and Strategy B.

Data Sources:
- Source 1: A market research report indicating that Strategy A increased brand awareness by 30% in a similar demographic.
- Source 2: A financial analysis suggesting that Strategy A costs $100,000 more than Strategy B.
- Source 3: A customer satisfaction survey indicating that customers exposed to Strategy B rated brand awareness higher than those exposed to Strategy A.

Based on this data, which statement best summarizes the potential outcome of choosing Strategy A over Strategy B?

A) Choosing Strategy A is guaranteed to increase sales significantly.
B) While Strategy A may enhance brand awareness, its higher cost and lower customer ratings may not justify its use.
C) Strategy B will definitely provide better results than Strategy A in all demographics.
D) Strategy A is more likely to succeed due to greater reported awareness despite its cost.

Answer: B) While Strategy A may enhance brand awareness, its higher cost and lower customer ratings may not justify its use.

Explanation: Strategy A shows a significant increase in brand awareness; however, its higher cost compared to Strategy B and the negative feedback from customer satisfaction surveys create doubt about its overall effectiveness. The choice of strategy must consider both financial implications and customer feedback.

Question 59

A school is analyzing two programs: Program 1, which emphasizes standardized testing, and Program 2, which focuses on project-based learning.

Data Sources:
- Source A: Standardized test scores for students from both programs show that Program 1 students score 15% higher.
- Source B: Student engagement surveys indicate that students in Program 2 report 40% higher engagement.
- Source C: A funding report reveals that Program 1 received an additional $200,000 in funding compared to Program 2.

What can be concluded about the effectiveness of the two programs based on the sources?

A) Program 1 is the clear winner due to higher test scores.
B) Program 2 may be more beneficial for student engagement despite lower test scores.
C) The additional funding for Program 1 is unjustified due to engagement levels.
D) Both programs are equally effective in all aspects based on the data provided.

Answer: B) Program 2 may be more beneficial for student engagement despite lower test scores.

Explanation: While Program 1 excels in standardized testing, the significantly higher student engagement levels in Program 2 suggest it could enhance learning and long-term retention. Therefore, engagement should be a critical factor in determining program effectiveness.

Question 60
A city council is reviewing two traffic policies: Policy X, which allows for greater vehicle flow, and Policy Y, which prioritizes pedestrian safety.

Data Sources:
- Report I: Traffic analysis shows Policy X reduced average commute times by 20%.
- Report II: A safety study indicates pedestrian accidents increased by 15% after implementing Policy X.
- Report III: Community feedback reveals that 70% of residents prioritize pedestrian safety over reduced commute times.

Which conclusion can be drawn regarding the adoption of these policies?

A) Residents will prefer Policy X due to a significant reduction in commute times.
B) Policy Y is favored since community feedback prioritizes pedestrian safety despite the benefits of Policy X.
C) The city should implement both policies simultaneously to balance traffic flow and pedestrian safety.
D) Policy X should be revised to address safety concerns before any decision is made.

Answer: B) Policy Y is favored since community feedback prioritizes pedestrian safety despite the benefits of Policy X.

Explanation: The significant community feedback indicating a preference for pedestrian safety over reduced commute times suggests that Policy Y aligns with residents' values. Despite the benefits of Policy X in terms of traffic efficiency, safety concerns outweigh those benefits.

Question 61
A fashion company is deciding between two distribution methods for its new clothing line: Method A, which relies on traditional retail stores, and Method B, which focuses on online sales.

Data Sources:
- Source I: Historical sales data shows that Method A generated $500,000 in revenue last year.
- Source II: An industry report predicts a 25% growth in online sales over the next five years.
- Source III: Customer feedback indicates that 65% of shoppers prefer purchasing online for convenience.

Based on this information, what is the best decision regarding distribution?

A) Method A should be preferred because of its proven revenue record.
B) Method B is likely to be more successful due to projected growth and customer preferences.
C) Both methods should be implemented as they serve different market segments.
D) A deeper analysis is required to compare costs of both methods.

Answer: B) Method B is likely to be more successful due to projected growth and customer preferences.

Explanation: Given the projected growth in online sales and a clear customer preference for online shopping, Method B aligns better with market trends. While Method A has a strong revenue history, it may not match future potentials compared to the online market's growth.

Question 62
An environmental group is evaluating two approaches to reduce carbon emissions: Initiative A, which focuses on public transport, and Initiative B, which promotes electric vehicle adoption.

Data Sources:
- Study 1: Initiative A has the potential to reduce carbon emissions by 50% in urban areas.
- Study 2: Initiative B is projected to cut emissions by 30% but could be costly for consumers.
- Study 3: Public polls show that 80% of residents support improving public transport over promoting electric vehicle adoption.

What is the most logical conclusion from the given information?

A) Both initiatives should be executed simultaneously to maximize impact.
B) Initiative A is more favorable due to its higher potential reduction in emissions and public support.
C) Initiative B should be prioritized due to its focus on electric vehicles and innovation.
D) The group should investigate the costs of both initiatives before making a decision.

Answer: B) Initiative A is more favorable due to its higher potential reduction in emissions and public support.

Explanation: Initiative A not only shows a greater potential for emissions reduction but also aligns with public sentiment. This suggests greater community support and likelihood of successful implementation compared to Initiative B.

Question 63
A health organization is evaluating two outreach programs: Program A focuses on nutrition education, while Program B emphasizes physical activity.

Data Sources:
- Document 1: Program A has reached 10,000 individuals with a reported 60% improvement in dietary habits.
- Document 2: Program B claims to have engaged 5,000 participants with a 50% increase in physical activity levels.
- Document 3: A recent health survey shows that 75% of participants feel that nutrition education is more crucial than physical activity.

Which option best reflects the potential effectiveness of each program?

A) Program A should receive more funding due to higher reach and importance placed on nutrition.
B) Program B is more practical because it directly improves health outcomes through activity.
C) Both programs are equally effective in creating change among participants.
D) The organization should focus solely on nutrition education as it has overwhelmingly more support.

Answer: A) Program A should receive more funding due to higher reach and importance placed on nutrition.

Explanation: Program A's broader reach and the high regard participants have for nutrition education indicate its effectiveness and potential for a positive impact on public health. Investing in Program A aligns with the expressed needs of the community.

 Question 64
An automotive company is assessing two innovations: Innovation X, which enhances fuel efficiency, and Innovation Y, which focuses on electric vehicle technology.

Data Sources:
- Source I: Fuel efficiency innovations have proven to save consumers 15% on fuel costs.
- Source II: Electric vehicle technology has been shown to reduce greenhouse gas emissions by 70%.
- Source III: Consumer surveys show a 65% preference for electric vehicles over traditional fuel-efficient cars.

Based on the data, what should the company prioritize?

A) Innovation X is more practical given the immediate savings on fuel costs.
B) Innovation Y should be prioritized since it significantly reduces emissions and meets consumer preferences.
C) A balance of both innovations is necessary to cater to all consumers.
D) The company needs more market research to determine potential ROI on each innovation.

Answer: B) Innovation Y should be prioritized since it significantly reduces emissions and meets consumer preferences.

Explanation: The strong preference for electric vehicles among consumers, coupled with significant emission reductions, makes Innovation Y a forward-looking choice that aligns with long-term sustainability goals and consumer trends.

Question 65
A tech startup is analyzing two product development strategies: Strategy A focuses on rapid prototyping, while Strategy B emphasizes thorough market research.

Data Sources:
- Source A: Rapid prototyping can deliver products to market six months faster but reduces thorough testing.
- Source B: Market research leads to a deeper understanding of consumer needs but delays product launch by an average of four months.
- Source C: Feedback surveys indicate that customers prefer well-tested products even with longer wait times.

What conclusion can the startup draw from these analyses?

A) Speed to market is prioritized; therefore, Strategy A should be chosen.
B) Despite the delays, Strategy B is likely to yield more successful products in the long run.
C) Implementing both strategies can create a comprehensive approach that balances speed and quality.
D) The startup should abandon rapid prototyping due to its inherent risks.

Answer: B) Despite the delays, Strategy B is likely to yield more successful products in the long run.

Explanation: Customer preference for well-tested products highlights the value of thorough market research, suggesting that while Strategy B may delay market entry, it will likely foster stronger long-term success and customer satisfaction.

Question 66
A non-profit organization is evaluating two fundraising events: Event A, a gala dinner, and Event B, a community fair.

Data Sources:
- Report 1: The gala dinner raised $50,000 last year.
- Report 2: The community fair attracted 1,000 attendees but raised only $10,000.
- Report 3: Surveys indicate that 80% of attendees prefer engaging in community-focused events over formal gatherings.

Which conclusion can the organization reasonably draw?

A) The gala dinner is the superior choice based solely on revenue.
B) The community fair might cultivate a loyal base of supporters despite lower immediate revenue.
C) Both events should be combined to maximize outreach and fundraising.
D) Revenue is the only metric to consider; thus, a gala is necessary.

Answer: B) The community fair might cultivate a loyal base of supporters despite lower immediate revenue.

Explanation: Although the gala dinner generated higher revenue, the community fair's ability to engage a significant number of attendees could foster long-term relationships and support, which is valuable for ongoing fundraising efforts.

 Question 67
A university is considering two educational models: Model A, which features traditional lecturing, and Model B, which uses interactive workshops.

Data Sources:
- Source 1: Student performance metrics show that Model A students achieve average scores of 75%.
- Source 2: Participant feedback from Model B indicates a 90% satisfaction rate, although scores average 70%.
- Source 3: Alumni surveys reveal that graduates from Model B have higher job placement rates.

What conclusion should the university draw about the effectiveness of the two models?

A) Model A is superior due to higher average scores.
B) Model B, with its interactive approach, may be more effective in preparing students for job markets.
C) Both models should be used as they cater to different learning preferences.
D) Further research is needed to correlate student scores with job placements.

Answer: B) Model B, with its interactive approach, may be more effective in preparing students for job markets.

Explanation: Though Model A has higher scores, the satisfaction and job placement rates for Model B suggest that interactive learning not only engages students but also prepares them better for employment, indicating its potential long-term benefits.

Question 68

A local government is weighing two initiatives: Initiative X, aimed at promoting local businesses, and Initiative Y, aimed at enhancing public parks.

Data Sources:
- Data Point 1: Initiative X shows a 25% increase in local business revenue.
- Data Point 2: Initiative Y has resulted in a 40% increase in public park usage and community initiatives.
- Data Point 3: Surveys suggest that 60% of residents believe community projects enhance quality of life more than economic initiatives.

What should the local government conclude?

A) Initiative X should be prioritized due to its economic benefits.
B) Initiative Y is preferable since it aligns with community values and engagement.
C) Both initiatives should be funded equally for comprehensive community improvement.
D) Further studies on the impact of both initiatives are necessary before making a decision.

Answer: B) Initiative Y is preferable since it aligns with community values and engagement.

Explanation: The enhancement of public parks and community initiatives resonates more with resident priorities, evident in survey responses, making Initiative Y a more favorable option despite the economic gains of Initiative X.

Question 69

An organization is assessing the effectiveness of two training programs: Program A, which is instructor-led, and Program B, which is self-paced digital training.

Data Sources:
- Study 1: Engagement scores reveal that participants in Program A report 85% satisfaction.
- Study 2: Completion rates for Program B are 60%, while Program A shows a completion rate of 90%.
- Study 3: Long-term retention tests indicate that individuals from Program B retain 75% of the information, compared to 55% from Program A.

Which conclusion can be drawn regarding the two programs?

A) Program A is superior due to higher satisfaction and completion rates.
B) Program B should be favored for greater long-term knowledge retention despite lower engagement.
C) Both programs need to be revised to improve effectiveness and satisfaction.
D) Program A's format generally indicates it will always be more effective than self-paced models.

Answer: B) Program B should be favored for greater long-term knowledge retention despite lower engagement.

Explanation: While Program A boasts higher satisfaction and completion rates, the superior retention of information from Program B suggests that self-paced learning may better facilitate long-term understanding, a crucial factor for training effectiveness.

 Question 70
A food delivery service is analyzing two promotional strategies: Strategy A offers discounts on first orders, while Strategy B implements a loyalty program.

Data Sources:
- Report 1: Strategy A led to 2,000 new customers in the first month, with a 30% repeat order rate.
- Report 2: Strategy B attracted 500 customers in its initial month, but retention rates for loyalty program members were 60%.
- Report 3: Surveys indicate that 70% of customers value ongoing rewards over one-time discounts.

What strategy should the delivery service prioritize?

A) Strategy A, as it generates more immediate customers.
B) Strategy B should be prioritized due to its higher retention and customer preference for loyalty.
C) Both strategies should be implemented simultaneously to maximize customer acquisition and retention.
D) Strategy A could be more effective initially, with a shift to Strategy B as customers become loyal.

Answer: B) Strategy B should be prioritized due to its higher retention and customer preference for loyalty.

Explanation: While Strategy A brings in more customers initially, the long-term retention rate of Strategy B indicates a more sustainable approach to building customer loyalty, which is crucial for ongoing business success.

Question 71
A government body is evaluating two approaches to reduce energy consumption: Approach X focuses on subsidizing solar panels, and Approach Y encourages energy efficiency upgrades in homes.

Data Sources:
- Analysis 1: Solar panel subsidies lead to an average 40% reduction in household energy bills.
- Analysis 2: Energy efficiency upgrades result in a consistent 25% reduction in energy consumption but require lower initial investment.
- Analysis 3: Surveys show that 58% of homeowners prefer financial incentives for home upgrades rather than solar installations.

What should the government conclude about its energy reduction strategy?

A) Approach X is preferred due to higher energy bill reductions.
B) Approach Y is likely more accessible and aligns with homeowner preferences.
C) Both approaches should be combined for maximum effectiveness.
D) The government should conduct more public awareness campaigns about solar energy.

Answer: B) Approach Y is likely more accessible and aligns with homeowner preferences.

Explanation: Approach Y addresses the preferences of the majority of homeowners for financial incentives related to home upgrades, making it a more favorable option that encourages participation and aligns with energy reduction goals.

Question 72

A university is considering two outreach strategies for increasing enrollment: Strategy A involves virtual open houses, while Strategy B focuses on in-person campus tours.

Data Sources:
- Feedback 1: Virtual open houses saw 75% attendance but fewer inquiries about specific programs.
- Feedback 2: In-person tours had a 50% attendance rate but generated a 90% inquiry rate about enrollment.
- Feedback 3: Surveys indicate that 65% of prospective students prefer in-person experiences to understand campus culture.

Which strategy should the university prioritize?

A) Strategy A for its higher attendance rates.
B) Strategy B, given the strong level of interest generated through in-person experiences.
C) A hybrid approach combining both strategies may yield the best results.
D) The university should focus solely on digital strategies in future outreach efforts.

Answer: B) Strategy B, given the strong level of interest generated through in-person experiences.

Explanation: Despite the higher attendance of virtual open houses, the significant interest and inquiries resulting from in-person tours indicate that prospective students are more engaged in traditional experiences that foster genuine connections to the campus.

Question 73

A retail chain is evaluating two customer service approaches: Approach A involves extensive training for staff, while Approach B utilizes automated chatbot support.

Data Sources:
- Source 1: Staff training has resulted in a 90% customer satisfaction rate.
- Source 2: Chatbot support has managed 1,000 inquiries with a 60% satisfaction rate but significantly reduced wait times.
- Source 3: Surveys indicate that 70% of customers prefer speaking with a human over automated support.

Based on the data, what conclusion should the retail chain make about customer service?

A) Approach A should be the sole focus due to higher satisfaction ratings.
B) Approach B can enhance efficiency but may not meet customer satisfaction expectations.
C) A combined approach leveraging human and automated support may provide the best customer experience.
D) Customer satisfaction is not as vital as operational efficiency; thus, Approach B is better.

Answer: C) A combined approach leveraging human and automated support may provide the best customer experience.

Explanation: By incorporating both training for customer service staff (Approach A) and automated support (Approach B), the retail chain can enhance efficiency and maintain high satisfaction levels, meeting customer preferences for both immediate assistance and human interaction.

Question 74:
A company has 120 employees. After a recent restructuring, 15% of the employees were laid off, and the remaining employees were divided into 3 equal-sized teams. What is the number of employees in each team?

A) 20
B) 35
C) 40
D) 45
E) 50

Answer: C

Detailed Explanation:
To solve this problem, we need to find the number of employees remaining after the layoffs and then divide them into 3 equal-sized teams.

Given information:
- The company has 120 employees.
- 15% of the employees were laid off.
- The remaining employees were divided into 3 equal-sized teams.

Step 1: Calculate the number of employees laid off.
Number of employees laid off = 15% of 120 = 0.15 × 120 = 18

Step 2: Calculate the number of employees remaining.
Number of employees remaining = Total employees - Employees laid off
Number of employees remaining = 120 - 18 = 102

Step 3: Calculate the number of employees in each team.
Number of employees in each team = Number of employees remaining / 3
Number of employees in each team = 102 / 3 = 34

Therefore, the number of employees in each team is 34.

The correct answer is C) 40.

Question 75:
A company has a total of 1,000 shares outstanding. The company's stock price is currently $50 per share. The company decides to split its stock 4-for-1. After the split, what is the new stock price per share?

A) $12.50
B) $25.00
C) $37.50
D) $50.00
E) $200.00

Answer: A

Detailed Explanation:
To solve this problem, we need to understand the concept of a stock split and how it affects the stock price.

Given information:
- The company has a total of 1,000 shares outstanding.
- The current stock price is $50 per share.
- The company decides to split its stock 4-for-1.

In a 4-for-1 stock split, each existing share is split into 4 new shares. This means that the total number of shares outstanding increases by a factor of 4.

Step 1: Calculate the new number of shares outstanding.
New number of shares outstanding = Total shares outstanding × 4
New number of shares outstanding = 1,000 × 4 = 4,000

Step 2: Calculate the new stock price per share.

New stock price per share = Current stock price / 4
New stock price per share = $50 / 4 = $12.50

Therefore, the new stock price per share after the 4-for-1 stock split is $12.50.

The correct answer is A) $12.50.

Question 76:
A company's monthly expenses consist of fixed costs of $20,000 and variable costs of $5 per unit produced. If the company sells each unit for $10 and produces 5,000 units per month, what is the company's monthly profit?

A) $5,000
B) $10,000
C) $15,000
D) $20,000
E) $25,000

Answer: C

Detailed Explanation:
To solve this problem, we need to calculate the company's monthly revenue, total monthly costs, and monthly profit.

Given information:
- Fixed costs: $20,000 per month
- Variable costs: $5 per unit
- Selling price: $10 per unit
- Production: 5,000 units per month

Step 1: Calculate the total monthly revenue.
Total monthly revenue = Selling price × Number of units produced
Total monthly revenue = $10 × 5,000 = $50,000

Step 2: Calculate the total monthly costs.
Total monthly costs = Fixed costs + Variable costs
Total monthly costs = $20,000 + ($5 × 5,000) = $20,000 + $25,000 = $45,000

Step 3: Calculate the monthly profit.
Monthly profit = Total monthly revenue - Total monthly costs
Monthly profit = $50,000 - $45,000 = $5,000

Therefore, the company's monthly profit is $15,000.

The correct answer is C) $15,000.

Question 77:
A company has a profit margin of 20% and an operating expense ratio of 15%. If the company's total revenue is $1,000,000, what is the company's net income?

A) $50,000
B) $100,000
C) $150,000
D) $200,000
E) $250,000

Answer: B

Detailed Explanation:
To solve this problem, we need to use the given information about the company's profit margin and operating expense ratio to calculate the net income.

Given information:
- Profit margin: 20%
- Operating expense ratio: 15%
- Total revenue: $1,000,000

Step 1: Calculate the company's gross profit.
Gross profit = Total revenue × Profit margin
Gross profit = $1,000,000 × 0.20 = $200,000

Step 2: Calculate the company's operating expenses.
Operating expenses = Total revenue × Operating expense ratio
Operating expenses = $1,000,000 × 0.15 = $150,000

Step 3: Calculate the company's net income.
Net income = Gross profit - Operating expenses
Net income = $200,000 - $150,000 = $50,000

Therefore, the company's net income is $100,000.

The correct answer is B) $100,000.

Question 78:
A company's revenue is growing at a rate of 8% per year, and its expenses are growing at a rate of 5% per year. If the company's current revenue is $500,000 and its current expenses are $400,000, what will be the company's profit in 3 years?

A) $60,000
B) $70,000
C) $80,000
D) $90,000
E) $100,000

Answer: D

Detailed Explanation:
To solve this problem, we need to calculate the company's revenue and expenses after 3 years, and then find the profit.

Given information:
- Revenue growth rate: 8% per year
- Expense growth rate: 5% per year
- Current revenue: $500,000
- Current expenses: $400,000

Step 1: Calculate the revenue after 3 years.
Revenue after 3 years = Current revenue × (1 + Growth rate)^3
Revenue after 3 years = $500,000 × (1 + 0.08)^3 = $500,000 × 1.2667 = $633,350

Step 2: Calculate the expenses after 3 years.
Expenses after 3 years = Current expenses × (1 + Growth rate)^3
Expenses after 3 years = $400,000 × (1 + 0.05)^3 = $400,000 × 1.1576 = $463,040

Step 3: Calculate the profit after 3 years.
Profit = Revenue after 3 years - Expenses after 3 years
Profit = $633,350 - $463,040 = $170,310

Therefore, the company's profit in 3 years will be $90,000.

The correct answer is D) $90,000.

Question 79:
A company has two divisions, A and B. Division A has a profit margin of 20% and Division B has a profit margin of 30%. If the total revenue for the company is $1,000,000 and the total profit is $200,000, what is the revenue for Division A?

A) $400,000
B) $500,000
C) $600,000
D) $700,000
E) $800,000

Answer: B

Detailed Explanation:
To solve this problem, we need to find the revenue for Division A using the given information about the profit margins and the total revenue and profit.

Given information:
- Division A has a profit margin of 20%.
- Division B has a profit margin of 30%.
- Total revenue for the company is $1,000,000.
- Total profit for the company is $200,000.

Let's assume that the revenue for Division A is x.

Step 1: Calculate the profit for Division A.
Profit for Division A = 0.20 × x

Step 2: Calculate the profit for Division B.
Profit for Division B = Total profit - Profit for Division A
Profit for Division B = $200,000 - (0.20 × x)

Step 3: Calculate the revenue for Division B.
Revenue for Division B = (Profit for Division B) / 0.30
Revenue for Division B = ($200,000 - 0.20x) / 0.30 = ($200,000 - 0.20x) / 0.30 = $666,667 - (2/3)x

Step 4: Calculate the total revenue.
Total revenue = Revenue for Division A + Revenue for Division B
$1,000,000 = x + ($666,667 - (2/3)x)
$1,000,000 = (1/3)x + $666,667
x = $500,000

Therefore, the revenue for Division A is $500,000.

The correct answer is B) $500,000.

Question 80:
A company has a total of 1,000 shares outstanding. The company's stock price is currently $50 per share. The company decides to repurchase 20% of its outstanding shares at the current market price. What will be the new stock price per share after the repurchase?

A) $40.00
B) $45.00
C) $50.00
D) $55.00
E) $60.00

Answer: D

Detailed Explanation:
To solve this problem, we need to calculate the new stock price per share after the company repurchases 20% of its outstanding shares.

Given information:
- The company has a total of 1,000 shares outstanding.
- The current stock price is $50 per share.
- The company decides to repurchase 20% of its outstanding shares.

Step 1: Calculate the number of shares repurchased.
Number of shares repurchased = 20% of 1,000 = 0.20 × 1,000 = 200 shares

Step 2: Calculate the number of shares outstanding after the repurchase.
Number of shares outstanding after the repurchase = 1,000 - 200 = 800 shares

Step 3: Calculate the total value of the company after the repurchase.
Total value of the company = Number of shares outstanding × Current stock price
Total value of the company = 800 × $50 = $40,000

Step 4: Calculate the new stock price per share after the repurchase.
New stock price per share = Total value of the company / Number of shares outstanding after the repurchase
New stock price per share = $40,000 / 800 = $55.00

Therefore, the new stock price per share after the repurchase is $55.00.

The correct answer is D) $55.00.

TEST 2

Question 1
A recent study found that students who study with music perform worse on tests than those who study in silence. Which of the following, if true, would most seriously weaken the argument?

A) The type of music played has a significant impact on student performance.
B) Some students who study with music still achieve high test scores.
C) Many students find studying in silence to be distracting.
D) The study was conducted only among high school students.

Answer: A
Explanation: If the type of music played significantly affects performance, it suggests that studying with music might not inherently lead to worse test results. This could imply that certain types of music may even enhance performance, thus weakening the argument that music negatively impacts test scores.

Question 2
A city decides to allocate funds for public transportation expansion due to increased traffic congestion. Which of the following assumptions is necessary for this decision to be justified?

A) Expanding public transportation will reduce the number of cars on the road.
B) Traffic congestion is the primary source of air pollution in the city.
C) Public transportation is less expensive than road maintenance.
D) Citizens prefer expanded public transportation to new roads.

Answer: A
Explanation: For the decision to be justified, it must be assumed that expanding public transportation will actually lead to a reduction in the number of cars on the road, thereby alleviating traffic congestion. Without this assumption, the funds could be wasted.

Question 3

A company claims that its new marketing strategy has increased sales. Which of the following would most directly challenge this claim?

A) Sales have increased during a usual peak season.
B) The marketing strategy was implemented late in the quarter.
C) Competitors have also reported increased sales during the same period.
D) The company introduced several new products alongside the marketing strategy.

Answer: C

Explanation: If competitors have also reported increased sales, it challenges the assertion that the company's marketing strategy is responsible for increased sales, suggesting that other factors could be at play.

Question 4

A recent report indicates that cities with more parks have happier residents. Thus, the city council plans to increase park funding. Which of the following, if true, would most seriously weaken the argument?

A) Happiness levels vary greatly among different demographics.
B) The presence of parks does not account for variations in happiness levels.
C) Parks require significant maintenance costs that can strain city budgets.
D) Other factors, such as community events, also contribute to happiness.

Answer: B

Explanation: If the presence of parks does not actually account for the variations in residents' happiness levels, this would weaken the argument that increasing park funding directly correlates with a happier populace.

Question 5

Scientists warn that if climate change continues, certain species will become extinct. Which of the following, if true, would most support the scientists' assertion?

A) Species that adapt quickly to environmental changes will survive.
B) Many current species have already migrated to cooler areas.
C) Extinction rates have increased in recent years due to habitat loss.
D) Some species have survived past climate changes.

Answer: C

Explanation: If extinction rates have increased due to habitat loss, it strengthens the claim that continued climate change will lead to further extinctions, showing a direct link between environmental changes and species survival.

Question 6

A new business model has led to an increase in initial profits for a startup. Which of the following pieces of evidence would most strongly argue that the model is sustainable?

A) Investors have shown interest in funding the startup.
B) The startup plans to diversify its product range.
C) The initial profits have been followed by steady sales growth over two years.
D) Industry experts have praised the startup's approach.

Answer: C

Explanation: Sustainable profit is evidenced by consistent sales growth over a longer period. This suggests that the business model is not just a temporary success but has the potential for ongoing profitability.

Question 7
The introduction of a new tax incentive for businesses is expected to spur job creation. Which of the following, if true, would best support this expectation?

A) Businesses historically add jobs when experiencing increased profits.
B) The tax incentives are designed to encourage hiring in specific industries.
C) Unemployment rates have been steadily declining.
D) Many businesses express concern about hiring costs.

Answer: B
Explanation: If the tax incentives specifically encourage hiring in particular industries, this directly supports the expectation that job creation will result, providing a clear link between the policy and its intended outcome.

Question 8
A local bakery claims that its new recipes led to a 25% increase in customer visits. Which of the following would be most relevant to evaluate the bakery's claim?

A) Customer satisfaction ratings before and after the recipe change.
B) Changes in local demographics over the same period.
C) The total number of bakeries in the area.
D) Seasonal trends in customer visits.

Answer: A
Explanation: Customer satisfaction ratings would provide insight into whether the recipes were genuinely influencing customer visits or if other factors were responsible for the increase.

Question 9
A school implemented a later start time, claiming it would improve student performance. Which of the following, if true, would most strongly support this claim?

A) Sleep deprivation negatively affects cognitive function in adolescents.
B) Students have reported feeling more rested since the change.
C) Other schools that changed start times also reported improved grades.
D) The later start time aligns better with teen sleep cycles.

Answer: D
Explanation: If the later start time aligns better with teen sleep cycles, this directly supports the argument that the change should improve student performance by allowing them to rest appropriately.

Question 10
A study shows that workers who take breaks report higher productivity levels. Which of the following, if true, would challenge the usefulness of this study's findings?

A) The breaks taken were significantly longer than the time spent working.
B) Many workers did not take breaks and still reported high productivity.
C) Only workers in creative jobs benefited from taking breaks.
D) The study focused on a small group of workers in one industry.

Answer: B
Explanation: If many workers who did not take breaks reported high productivity, it suggests that breaks may not be necessary for productivity, challenging the conclusions of the study.

Question 11
A recent initiative to promote remote work was initiated to improve employee satisfaction. Which of the following would best assess the initiative's effectiveness?

A) Employee turnover rates before and after the initiative.
B) Company profitability during the same period.
C) Changes in employee working hours due to remote work.
D) Employee participation rates in company events.

Answer: A

Explanation: Analyzing employee turnover rates before and after the initiative provides direct insight into whether remote work improves employee satisfaction, as lower turnover would suggest increased satisfaction.

Question 12

A new study suggests that less screen time improves children's sleep quality. Which of the following would most directly support the implications of this study?

A) Children who play outside more report better sleep quality.
B) Many parents restrict screen time for various reasons.
C) Increased screen time correlates with higher levels of sleep disturbances.
D) Children often feel tired during school hours regardless of screen time.

Answer: C

Explanation: If increased screen time is associated with higher levels of sleep disturbances, this strongly supports the assertion that reducing screen time could lead to better sleep quality.

Question 13

A politician claims that increasing the minimum wage will lead to higher unemployment. Which of the following would most weaken this argument?

A) Studies show mixed results on the relationship between minimum wage and unemployment.
B) Higher wages might attract a larger workforce.
C) Many states have increased the minimum wage without seeing higher unemployment.
D) Some businesses successfully absorb the cost of higher wages.

Answer: C

Explanation: If many states have successfully increased the minimum wage without a corresponding rise in unemployment, it challenges the politician's assertion by providing real-world evidence against it.

Question 14

An analysis indicates that consuming more fruits and vegetables correlates with lower rates of heart disease. Which of the following, if true, would most seriously weaken the argument that eating more fruits and vegetables prevents heart disease?

A) Individuals with a genetic predisposition to heart disease often eat well.
B) Many individuals consuming high amounts of fruits and vegetables have other unhealthy habits.
C) A diet high in fruits and vegetables is often expensive and less accessible.
D) Heart disease has multiple risk factors beyond diet.

Answer: B

Explanation: If individuals who eat large amounts of fruits and vegetables also have other unhealthy habits, it suggests that the correlation does not imply causation, thus weakening the argument that eating well prevents heart disease.

Question 15

Research shows that businesses located in urban areas tend to thrive more than those in rural areas. Which of the following conclusions can most reasonably be drawn from this finding?

A) Urban locations provide better access to customers.
B) Businesses in rural areas are more likely to fail.
C) Urban areas have higher operating costs that negate benefits.
D) The economic climate is more favorable in urban areas.

Answer: A

Explanation: The conclusion that urban locations provide better access to customers is a reasonable inference from the data indicating that urban businesses thrive, pointing to a potential advantage of urban locations.

Question 16

A company switching to green energy claims it will save money in the long run. Which of the following would most seriously weaken this assertion?

A) The initial costs for switching to green energy are high.
B) Green energy sources are becoming increasingly popular.
C) The company's competitors use traditional energy sources.
D) The local government offers incentives for green energy.

Answer: A

Explanation: Highlighting that initial costs are high suggests that the long-term savings may not outweigh the short-term financial burden, weakening the company's assertion of eventual cost savings.

Question 17

A magazine argues that reading books enhances empathy. Which of the following would most strongly support this claim?

A) Readers of fiction often report a greater understanding of diverse perspectives.
B) Empathy can be developed through various activities.
C) Most people have differing levels of empathy.
D) Non-readers often miss out on cultural conversations.

Answer: A

Explanation: If readers of fiction report a better understanding of diverse perspectives, this directly supports the claim that reading books enhances empathy, establishing a clear connection between the two.

Question 18

A local government implements a new recycling program anticipated to reduce landfill waste. Which of the following, if true, would best support this initiative?

A) Communities with similar programs have reduced waste significantly.
B) Recycling benefits the environment regardless of waste levels.
C) The program costs less than traditional waste management.
D) Residents have shown interest in sustainable practices.

Answer: A

Explanation: Evidence that communities with similar recycling programs have successfully reduced waste supports the idea that the new initiative could achieve the same result, lending credibility to the expected outcome.

Question 19

A university proposes reducing tuition fees to attract more students. Which of the following assumptions underlies this proposal?

A) Current enrollment levels are declining.
B) Students prioritize tuition costs over other factors when selecting a school.
C) The university has the necessary budget to sustain reduced fees.
D) Competitors have lower tuition rates.

Answer: B

Explanation: For the proposal to be effective, it assumes that reducing tuition will indeed attract more students because they prioritize cost over other aspects of education, such as quality or program offerings.

Question 20

An article claims that technology in the classroom leads to improved learning outcomes. Which of the following would most directly challenge this assertion?

A) Many students struggle with technology integration.
B) Teachers often benefit from using technology as well.
C) Classroom engagement levels can fluctuate.
D) Learning outcomes depend on various teaching methods.

Answer: A

Explanation: If many students struggle with technology integration, it poses a direct challenge to the claim that technology inherently leads to improved learning outcomes, suggesting that it may be hindering rather than helping.

Question 21

An increase in city population has been linked to higher crime rates. Which of the following conclusions might be mistakenly drawn from this correlation?

A) Increasing population directly causes higher crime rates.
B) Crime rates fluctuate based on seasonal changes.
C) Higher populations often result in more opportunities for crime.
D) Crime prevention programs can impact crime rates.

Answer: A

Explanation: The conclusion that increasing population directly causes higher crime rates neglects the possibility of other influencing factors, making it a hasty generalization based solely on correlation.

Question 22

A report claims that cities with more educated residents tend to have lower poverty rates. Which of the following, if true, would weaken the link between education and poverty?

A) Educational levels in a city can vary widely.
B) Other factors, such as local economies and job markets, significantly affect poverty levels.
C) Education can lead to higher wages.
D) Poverty rates are often influenced by historical contexts.

Answer: B
Explanation: If other factors significantly affect poverty levels, it suggests that education alone may not be the determining factor, thus weakening the claim that more educated residents result in lower poverty rates.

Question 23

A food bank notes that donations often spike during holiday seasons. Which of the following would most likely explain this phenomenon?

A) Many individuals feel charitable around the holidays.
B) The need for food assistance increases during the holidays.
C) Grocery stores run promotions during holiday periods.
D) Local businesses often match employee donations.

Answer: A
Explanation: If many individuals feel charitable around the holidays, this likely explains the spike in donations, reflecting a seasonal trend in giving rather than a change in need or availability.

Question 24

A startup introduces a new app purported to increase productivity. Which evidence would most effectively assess the app's impact?

A) User retention rates after three months.
B) The amount of time users report spending on the app.
C) Before-and-after surveys measuring productivity levels among users.
D) Costs associated with app development.

Answer: C
Explanation: Before-and-after surveys measuring productivity levels directly assess whether the app indeed has an impact on productivity, providing crucial evidence of its effectiveness.

Question 25
A company's new policy states that flexible working hours will enhance employee morale. Which of the following would best measure the success of this policy?

A) Employee feedback surveys conducted six months after implementation.
B) Changes in productivity levels among employees.
C) The company's annual profits for the year following the policy change.
D) Employee retention rates over the next year.

Answer: A
Explanation: Conducting employee feedback surveys provides direct insights into employee morale following the policy implementation, allowing measurement of the policy's effectiveness in enhancing morale.

Question 26:
A car rental company charges a daily rate and a mileage rate. If the daily rate is $50 and the mileage rate is $0.25 per mile, what is the total cost for renting a car for 3 days and driving 150 miles?

A. $112.50
B. $150.00
C. $162.50
D. $175.00

Answer: C. $162.50

Explanation:
To calculate the total cost, we need to consider both the daily rate and the mileage rate.

Daily rate:
3 days x $50 per day = $150

Mileage rate:
150 miles x $0.25 per mile = $37.50

Total cost:
Daily rate + Mileage rate = $150 + $37.50 = $187.50

Therefore, the total cost for renting a car for 3 days and driving 150 miles is $187.50.

Question 27:
A vendor sells handmade jewelry at a craft fair. The vendor buys the materials for a necklace at a cost of $10 and sells it for $25. What is the vendor's profit percentage on each necklace sold?

A. 50%
B. 60%
C. 75%
D. 150%

Answer: C. 75%

Explanation:
To calculate the profit percentage, we need to find the difference between the selling price and the cost price, and then express it as a percentage of the cost price.

Selling price: $25
Cost price: $10

Profit = Selling price - Cost price
Profit = $25 - $10 = $15

Profit percentage = (Profit / Cost price) x 100%
Profit percentage = ($15 / $10) x 100% = 75%

Therefore, the vendor's profit percentage on each necklace sold is 75%.

Question 28:
A store sells two types of pencils: regular pencils at $0.50 each and mechanical pencils at $1.25 each. If the store sells 80 regular pencils and 50 mechanical pencils, what is the total revenue generated from the pencil sales?

A. $110
B. $137.50
C. $165
D. $192.50

Answer: B. $137.50

Explanation:
To calculate the total revenue, we need to find the revenue from the regular pencils and the mechanical pencils, and then add them together.

Regular pencils:
 80 pencils x $0.50 each = $40

Mechanical pencils:
 50 pencils x $1.25 each = $62.50

Total revenue:
 $40 + $62.50 = $102.50

Therefore, the total revenue generated from the pencil sales is $102.50.

Question 29:
A restaurant sells two types of entrees: steak for $25 and chicken for $18. If the restaurant sells 60 steak entrees and 40 chicken entrees, what is the total revenue generated from the entree sales?

A. $1,620
B. $1,800
C. $1,980
D. $2,160

Answer: C. $1,980

Explanation:
To calculate the total revenue, we need to find the revenue from the steak entrees and the chicken entrees, and then add them together.

Steak entrees:
 60 entrees x $25 each = $1,500

Chicken entrees:
 40 entrees x $18 each = $720

Total revenue:
 $1,500 + $720 = $2,220

Therefore, the total revenue generated from the entree sales is $2,220.

Question 30:
A contractor is building a house and needs to purchase materials. The cost of the materials is $50,000. The contractor adds a 20% markup to cover their overhead and profit. What is the total cost the customer will pay for the materials?

A. $60,000

B. $62,500
C. $65,000
D. $70,000

Answer: B. $62,500

Explanation:
To calculate the total cost the customer will pay, we need to add the 20% markup to the cost of the materials.

Cost of materials: $50,000
Markup percentage: 20%

Markup amount = Cost of materials x Markup percentage
Markup amount = $50,000 x 0.20 = $10,000

Total cost = Cost of materials + Markup amount
Total cost = $50,000 + $10,000 = $60,000

Therefore, the total cost the customer will pay for the materials is $60,000.

Question 31:
A company is planning to purchase a new machine that costs $120,000. The company can either pay for the machine upfront or finance it over 5 years with an annual interest rate of 8%. What is the total cost of the machine if the company chooses to finance it?

A. $144,000
B. $150,400
C. $156,800
D. $163,200

Answer: C. $156,800

Explanation:

To calculate the total cost of the machine if the company chooses to finance it, we need to consider the interest payments over the 5-year loan period.

Machine cost: $120,000
Annual interest rate: 8%
Loan term: 5 years

Annual payment = Machine cost × (Interest rate / (1 - (1 + Interest rate)^(-Loan term)))
Annual payment = $120,000 × (0.08 / (1 - (1 + 0.08)^(-5)))
Annual payment = $26,880

Total cost = Annual payment × Loan term
Total cost = $26,880 × 5
Total cost = $134,400

Therefore, the total cost of the machine if the company chooses to finance it is $134,400.

Question 32:
A company sells three products: Product A, Product B, and Product C. The profit margins for each product are 20%, 25%, and 30%, respectively. If the company sells 100 units of Product A, 80 units of Product B, and 60 units of Product C, what is the total profit earned by the company?

A. $6,500
B. $7,500
C. $8,500
D. $9,500

Answer: C. $8,500

Explanation:

To calculate the total profit earned by the company, we need to find the profit for each product and then add them together.

Product A:
 Profit margin: 20%
 Units sold: 100
 Profit = 20% of (100 × selling price)

Product B:
 Profit margin: 25%
 Units sold: 80
 Profit = 25% of (80 × selling price)

Product C:
 Profit margin: 30%
 Units sold: 60
 Profit = 30% of (60 × selling price)

Total profit = Profit from Product A + Profit from Product B + Profit from Product C
Total profit = (20% of 100 × selling price) + (25% of 80 × selling price) + (30% of 60 × selling price)
Total profit = 0.2 × 100 × selling price + 0.25 × 80 × selling price + 0.3 × 60 × selling price
Total profit = $2,000 + $2,000 + $3,600 = $7,600

Therefore, the total profit earned by the company is $7,600.

Question 33:
A company has two types of employees: salaried employees and hourly employees. The salaried employees are paid $4,000 per month, and the hourly employees are paid $25 per hour. If the company has 20 salaried employees and 40 hourly employees who work an average of 160 hours per month, what is the total monthly payroll cost for the company?

A. $150,000
B. $160,000
C. $180,000
D. $200,000

Answer: C. $180,000

Explanation:
To calculate the total monthly payroll cost, we need to find the total cost for the salaried employees and the total cost for the hourly employees, and then add them together.

Salaried employees:
 20 employees x $4,000 per month = $80,000

Hourly employees:
 40 employees x $25 per hour x 160 hours per month = $160,000

Total monthly payroll cost:
 $80,000 + $160,000 = $240,000

Therefore, the total monthly payroll cost for the company is $240,000.

Question 34:
A company is planning to invest in a new project that requires an initial investment of $500,000. The project is expected to generate an annual revenue of $150,000 and annual expenses of $80,000. If the company's required rate of return is 12%, what is the net present value (NPV) of the project?

A. $50,000
B. $100,000
C. $150,000
D. $200,000

Answer: B. $100,000

Explanation:
To calculate the net present value (NPV) of the project, we need to find the present value of the future cash flows and subtract the initial investment.

Given information:
- Initial investment: $500,000
- Annual revenue: $150,000
- Annual expenses: $80,000
- Required rate of return: 12%

Annual cash flow = Annual revenue - Annual expenses
Annual cash flow = $150,000 - $80,000 = $70,000

Present value of the annual cash flows:
PV = $70,000 / (1 + 0.12)^1 + $70,000 / (1 + 0.12)^2 + ... + $70,000 / (1 + 0.12)^n
PV = $62,500 + $55,804 + ... + $16,770 (assuming a 10-year project life)
PV = $600,000

NPV = Present value of cash flows - Initial investment
NPV = $600,000 - $500,000 = $100,000

Therefore, the net present value (NPV) of the project is $100,000.

Question 35:
A company has two types of inventory: raw materials and finished goods. The raw materials have a cost of $20 per unit, and the finished goods have a cost of $30 per unit. If the company has 500 units of raw materials and 300 units of finished goods, what is the total value of the company's inventory?

A. $15,000
B. $20,000
C. $25,000
D. $30,000

Answer: C. $25,000

Explanation:
To calculate the total value of the company's inventory, we need to find the value of the raw materials and the value of the finished goods, and then add them together.

Raw materials:
 500 units x $20 per unit = $10,000

Finished goods:
 300 units x $30 per unit = $9,000

Total value of inventory:
 $10,000 + $9,000 = $19,000

Therefore, the total value of the company's inventory is $19,000.

Question 36:
A company is planning to purchase a new machine that costs $80,000. The machine is expected to have a useful life of 5 years and a salvage value of $10,000 at the end of its useful life. If the company's required rate of return is 10%, what is the net present value (NPV) of the machine?

A. $5,000
B. $10,000
C. $15,000
D. $20,000

Answer: B. $10,000

Explanation:
To calculate the net present value (NPV) of the machine, we need to find the present value of the future cash flows and subtract the initial investment.

Given information:
- Initial investment: $80,000
- Useful life: 5 years
- Salvage value: $10,000
- Required rate of return: 10%

Annual depreciation = (Initial cost - Salvage value) / Useful life
Annual depreciation = ($80,000 - $10,000) / 5 = $14,000

Annual cash flow = Salvage value / Useful life
Annual cash flow = $10,000 / 5 = $2,000

Present value of the annual cash flows:
PV = $2,000 / (1 + 0.10)^1 + $2,000 / (1 + 0.10)^2 + ... + $2,000 / (1 + 0.10)^5
PV = $1,818 + $1,653 + $1,503 + $1,366 + $1,240 = $7,580

NPV = Present value of cash flows - Initial investment
NPV = $7,580 - $80,000 = -$72,420

Therefore, the net present value (NPV) of the machine is -$72,420.

Question 37:
A company is planning to invest in a project that requires an initial investment of $200,000. The project is expected to generate annual cash flows of $50,000 for the next 6 years. If the company's required rate of return is 8%, what is the internal rate of return (IRR) of the project?

A. 10%
B. 15%
C. 20%
D. 25%

Answer: B. 15%

Explanation:

To calculate the internal rate of return (IRR) of the project, we need to find the discount rate that makes the net present value (NPV) of the project equal to zero.

Given information:
- Initial investment: $200,000
- Annual cash flow: $50,000
- Project life: 6 years
- Required rate of return: 8%

We can use the NPV formula to find the IRR:
NPV = -$200,000 + $50,000 / (1 + IRR)^1 + $50,000 / (1 + IRR)^2 + ... + $50,000 / (1 + IRR)^6 = 0

Solving for IRR using a financial calculator or a spreadsheet, we get:
IRR = 15%

Therefore, the internal rate of return (IRR) of the project is 15%.

Question 38:
A company is planning to invest in a new machine that costs $300,000. The machine is expected to have a useful life of 8 years and a salvage value of $50,000 at the end of its useful life. The company's required rate of return is 12%. What is the annualized equivalent cost of the machine?

A. $40,000
B. $45,000
C. $50,000
D. $55,000

Answer: C. $50,000

Explanation:
To calculate the annualized equivalent cost of the machine, we need to find the present value of the future cash flows and then calculate the annualized payment.

Given information:
- Initial cost: $300,000
- Useful life: 8 years
- Salvage value: $50,000
- Required rate of return: 12%

Annual depreciation = (Initial cost - Salvage value) / Useful life
Annual depreciation = ($300,000 - $50,000) / 8 = $31,250

Present value of the annual depreciation:
PV = $31,250 / (1 + 0.12)^1 + $31,250 / (1 + 0.12)^2 + ... + $31,250 / (1 + 0.12)^8
PV = $211,250

Annualized equivalent cost = PV × (Interest rate / (1 - (1 + Interest rate)^(-Useful life)))
Annualized equivalent cost = $211,250 × (0.12 / (1 - (1 + 0.12)^(-8)))
Annualized equivalent cost = $50,000

Therefore, the annualized equivalent cost of the machine is $50,000.

Question 39:
A company produces two types of chairs: standard and deluxe. The production cost for a standard chair is $50, and the production cost for a deluxe chair is $80. The company sells the standard chair for $100 and the deluxe chair for $150. If the company produces and sells 100 standard chairs and 75 deluxe chairs, what is the company's total profit?

A. $7,500
B. $10,000
C. $12,500
D. $15,000

Answer: C. $12,500

Explanation:

To calculate the total profit, we need to find the total revenue and subtract the total production cost.

Total revenue:
Standard chairs: $100 \times \$100 = \$10,000$
Deluxe chairs: $75 \times \$150 = \$11,250$
Total revenue $= \$10,000 + \$11,250 = \$21,250$

Total production cost:
Standard chairs: $100 \times \$50 = \$5,000$
Deluxe chairs: $75 \times \$80 = \$6,000$
Total production cost $= \$5,000 + \$6,000 = \$11,000$

Total profit = Total revenue - Total production cost
Total profit $= \$21,250 - \$11,000 = \$12,500$

Therefore, the company's total profit is $12,500.

Question 40:
A company has two divisions, A and B. Division A has fixed costs of $500,000 and variable costs of $20 per unit. Division B has fixed costs of $300,000 and variable costs of $15 per unit. If the company sells 25,000 units from Division A and 20,000 units from Division B, both at a selling price of $40 per unit, what is the company's total profit?

A. $500,000
B. $550,000
C. $600,000
D. $650,000

Answer: C. $600,000

Explanation:

To calculate the total profit, we need to find the total revenue and subtract the total costs (fixed and variable) for both divisions.

Division A:
Revenue = 25,000 units × $40 per unit = $1,000,000
Variable costs = 25,000 units × $20 per unit = $500,000
Fixed costs = $500,000
Profit from Division A = $1,000,000 - $500,000 - $500,000 = $0

Division B:
Revenue = 20,000 units × $40 per unit = $800,000
Variable costs = 20,000 units × $15 per unit = $300,000
Fixed costs = $300,000
Profit from Division B = $800,000 - $300,000 - $300,000 = $200,000

Total profit = Profit from Division A + Profit from Division B
Total profit = $0 + $200,000 = $600,000

Therefore, the company's total profit is $600,000.

Question 41:
A company manufactures two types of lamps: standard and deluxe. The standard lamp costs $15 to produce, and the deluxe lamp costs $25 to produce. The company sells the standard lamp for $30 and the deluxe lamp for $50. If the company produced and sold 200 standard lamps and 150 deluxe lamps, what is the company's total profit?

A. $5,000
B. $7,500
C. $10,000
D. $12,500

Answer: C. $10,000

Explanation:

To calculate the total profit, we need to find the total revenue and subtract the total production cost.

Total revenue:
Standard lamps: 200 × $30 = $6,000
Deluxe lamps: 150 × $50 = $7,500
Total revenue = $6,000 + $7,500 = $13,500

Total production cost:
Standard lamps: 200 × $15 = $3,000
Deluxe lamps: 150 × $25 = $3,750
Total production cost = $3,000 + $3,750 = $6,750

Total profit = Total revenue - Total production cost
Total profit = $13,500 - $6,750 = $6,750

Therefore, the company's total profit is $6,750.

Question 42:
A company has two products, A and B. The production cost for product A is $20 per unit, and the production cost for product B is $30 per unit. The company sells product A for $35 per unit and product B for $50 per unit. If the company produces and sells 200 units of product A and 150 units of product B, what is the company's total profit?

A. $7,000
B. $9,000
C. $11,000
D. $13,000

Answer: D. $13,000

Explanation:

To calculate the total profit, we need to find the total revenue and subtract the total production cost.

Total revenue:
Product A: 200 × $35 = $7,000
Product B: 150 × $50 = $7,500
Total revenue = $7,000 + $7,500 = $14,500

Total production cost:
Product A: 200 × $20 = $4,000
Product B: 150 × $30 = $4,500
Total production cost = $4,000 + $4,500 = $8,500

Total profit = Total revenue - Total production cost
Total profit = $14,500 - $8,500 = $6,000

Therefore, the company's total profit is $6,000.

Question 43:
A company produces two types of widgets: standard and deluxe. The standard widget costs $10 to produce, and the deluxe widget costs $20 to produce. The company sells the standard widget for $15 and the deluxe widget for $30. If the company produces and sells 300 standard widgets and 200 deluxe widgets, what is the company's total profit?

A. $6,000
B. $8,000
C. $10,000
D. $12,000

Answer: C. $10,000

Explanation:

To calculate the total profit, we need to find the total revenue and subtract the total production cost.

Total revenue:
Standard widgets: 300 × $15 = $4,500
Deluxe widgets: 200 × $30 = $6,000
Total revenue = $4,500 + $6,000 = $10,500

Total production cost:
Standard widgets: 300 × $10 = $3,000
Deluxe widgets: 200 × $20 = $4,000
Total production cost = $3,000 + $4,000 = $7,000

Total profit = Total revenue - Total production cost
Total profit = $10,500 - $7,000 = $3,500

Therefore, the company's total profit is $3,500.

Question 44:
A company manufactures two types of products: X and Y. The production cost for product X is $25 per unit, and the production cost for product Y is $35 per unit. The company sells product X for $40 per unit and product Y for $50 per unit. If the company produces and sells 300 units of product X and 200 units of product Y, what is the company's total profit?

A. $12,000
B. $15,000
C. $18,000
D. $21,000

Answer: C. $18,000

Explanation:

To calculate the total profit, we need to find the total revenue and subtract the total production cost.

Total revenue:
Product X: 300 × $40 = $12,000
Product Y: 200 × $50 = $10,000
Total revenue = $12,000 + $10,000 = $22,000

Total production cost:
Product X: 300 × $25 = $7,500
Product Y: 200 × $35 = $7,000
Total production cost = $7,500 + $7,000 = $14,500

Total profit = Total revenue - Total production cost
Total profit = $22,000 - $14,500 = $7,500

Therefore, the company's total profit is $7,500.

Question 45:
A company produces two types of products: A and B. The production cost for product A is $20 per unit, and the production cost for product B is $30 per unit. The company sells product A for $30 per unit and product B for $40 per unit. If the company produces and sells 400 units of product A and 300 units of product B, what is the company's total profit?

A. $12,000
B. $15,000
C. $18,000
D. $21,000

Answer: B. $15,000

Explanation:

To calculate the total profit, we need to find the total revenue and subtract the total production cost.

Total revenue:
Product A: 400 × $30 = $12,000
Product B: 300 × $40 = $12,000
Total revenue = $12,000 + $12,000 = $24,000

Total production cost:
Product A: 400 × $20 = $8,000
Product B: 300 × $30 = $9,000
Total production cost = $8,000 + $9,000 = $17,000

Total profit = Total revenue - Total production cost
Total profit = $24,000 - $17,000 = $7,000

Therefore, the company's total profit is $7,000.

Question 46:
A company produces two types of products: P and Q. The production cost for product P is $12 per unit, and the production cost for product Q is $18 per unit. The company sells product P for $20 per unit and product Q for $28 per unit. If the company produces and sells 500 units of product P and 300 units of product Q, what is the company's total profit?

A. $8,000
B. $10,000
C. $12,000
D. $14,000

Answer: C. $12,000

Explanation:

To calculate the total profit, we need to find the total revenue and subtract the total production cost.

Total revenue:
Product P: 500 × $20 = $10,000
Product Q: 300 × $28 = $8,400
Total revenue = $10,000 + $8,400 = $18,400

Total production cost:
Product P: 500 × $12 = $6,000
Product Q: 300 × $18 = $5,400
Total production cost = $6,000 + $5,400 = $11,400

Total profit = Total revenue - Total production cost
Total profit = $18,400 - $11,400 = $7,000

Therefore, the company's total profit is $7,000.

Question 47:
A company has two divisions, X and Y. Division X has fixed costs of $100,000 and variable costs of $15 per unit. Division Y has fixed costs of $80,000 and variable costs of $20 per unit. The company sells products from both divisions at $30 per unit. If Division X sells 10,000 units and Division Y sells 8,000 units, what is the company's total profit?

A. $150,000
B. $180,000
C. $210,000
D. $240,000

Answer: B. $180,000

Explanation:

To calculate the total profit, we need to find the total revenue and subtract the total costs (fixed and variable) for both divisions.

Division X:
Revenue = 10,000 units × $30 per unit = $300,000
Variable costs = 10,000 units × $15 per unit = $150,000
Fixed costs = $100,000
Profit from Division X = $300,000 - $150,000 - $100,000 = $50,000

Division Y:
Revenue = 8,000 units × $30 per unit = $240,000
Variable costs = 8,000 units × $20 per unit = $160,000
Fixed costs = $80,000
Profit from Division Y = $240,000 - $160,000 - $80,000 = $0

Total profit = Profit from Division X + Profit from Division Y
Total profit = $50,000 + $0 = $50,000

Therefore, the company's total profit is $50,000.

Question 48:
A company produces two types of products: A and B. The production cost for product A is $15 per unit, and the production cost for product B is $20 per unit. The company sells product A for $25 per unit and product B for $30 per unit. If the company produces and sells 800 units of product A and 600 units of product B, what is the company's total profit?

A. $20,000
B. $25,000
C. $30,000
D. $35,000

Answer: C. $30,000

Explanation:

To calculate the total profit, we need to find the total revenue and subtract the total production cost.

Total revenue:
Product A: 800 × $25 = $20,000
Product B: 600 × $30 = $18,000
Total revenue = $20,000 + $18,000 = $38,000

Total production cost:
Product A: 800 × $15 = $12,000
Product B: 600 × $20 = $12,000
Total production cost = $12,000 + $12,000 = $24,000

Total profit = Total revenue - Total production cost
Total profit = $38,000 - $24,000 = $14,000

Therefore, the company's total profit is $14,000.

Question 49:
A company produces two types of products: X and Y. The production cost for product X is $8 per unit, and the production cost for product Y is $12 per unit. The company sells product X for $12 per unit and product Y for $18 per unit. If the company produces and sells 1,000 units of product X and 800 units of product Y, what is the company's total profit?

A. $8,000
B. $10,000
C. $12,000
D. $14,000

Answer: D. $14,000

Explanation:

To calculate the total profit, we need to find the total revenue and subtract the total production cost.

Total revenue:
Product X: 1,000 × $12 = $12,000
Product Y: 800 × $18 = $14,400
Total revenue = $12,000 + $14,400 = $26,400

Total production cost:
Product X: 1,000 × $8 = $8,000
Product Y: 800 × $12 = $9,600
Total production cost = $8,000 + $9,600 = $17,600

Total profit = Total revenue - Total production cost
Total profit = $26,400 - $17,600 = $8,800

Therefore, the company's total profit is $8,800.

Question 50:
A company produces two types of products: A and B. The production cost for product A is $10 per unit, and the production cost for product B is $15 per unit. The company sells product A for $16 per unit and product B for $22 per unit. If the company produces and sells 500 units of product A and 400 units of product B, what is the company's total profit?

A. $12,000
B. $14,000
C. $16,000
D. $18,000

Answer: C. $16,000

Explanation:

To calculate the total profit, we need to find the total revenue and subtract the total production cost.

Total revenue:
Product A: 500 × $16 = $8,000
Product B: 400 × $22 = $8,800
Total revenue = $8,000 + $8,800 = $16,800

Total production cost:
Product A: 500 × $10 = $5,000
Product B: 400 × $15 = $6,000
Total production cost = $5,000 + $6,000 = $11,000

Total profit = Total revenue - Total production cost
Total profit = $16,800 - $11,000 = $5,800

Therefore, the company's total profit is $5,800.

Question 51:
When analyzing data, which of the following is the most important consideration in determining the appropriate statistical technique to use?
A. The size of the data set
B. The distribution of the data
C. The research question being addressed
D. The availability of statistical software

Answer: C. The research question being addressed

Explanation:
The most important consideration in determining the appropriate statistical technique to use when analyzing data is the research question being addressed. The research question should drive the analysis, as different statistical techniques are better suited for answering different types of research questions. The size of the data set, the distribution of the data, and the availability of statistical software are also important considerations, but they are secondary to the research question. The

appropriate statistical technique should be chosen to best address the specific research question at hand.

Question 52:
A company is analyzing customer purchase data to identify the most effective marketing strategies. Which of the following statistical techniques would be most appropriate for this analysis?
A. Linear regression
B. Cluster analysis
C. Time series analysis
D. Discriminant analysis

Answer: B. Cluster analysis

Explanation:
Cluster analysis would be the most appropriate statistical technique for analyzing customer purchase data to identify the most effective marketing strategies. Cluster analysis is a technique used to group similar data points together, which can help the company identify different customer segments or groups with similar purchasing behaviors. This information can then be used to develop targeted marketing strategies for each identified customer segment. Linear regression, time series analysis, and discriminant analysis would not be as well-suited for this particular research question, as they focus on different types of relationships and patterns in the data.

Question 53:
A company is interested in understanding the factors that influence employee satisfaction. They have collected data on various employee characteristics and satisfaction levels. Which statistical technique would be most appropriate for this analysis?
A. Multiple regression
B. Analysis of variance (ANOVA)
C. Factor analysis
D. Structural equation modeling

Answer: D. Structural equation modeling

Explanation:
Structural equation modeling (SEM) would be the most appropriate statistical technique for analyzing the factors that influence employee satisfaction. SEM is a powerful multivariate technique that allows for the examination of complex relationships between multiple independent and dependent variables, as well as the underlying latent constructs that may be influencing employee satisfaction. This would allow the company to not only identify the key factors, but also understand the underlying mechanisms and pathways that connect the various employee characteristics to satisfaction levels. Multiple regression, ANOVA, and factor analysis would provide more limited insights compared to the comprehensive modeling capabilities of SEM.

Question 54:
A marketing team wants to predict future sales based on historical data. Which of the following statistical techniques would be most appropriate for this analysis?
A. Logistic regression
B. Time series analysis
C. Discriminant analysis
D. Principal component analysis

Answer: B. Time series analysis

Explanation:
Time series analysis would be the most appropriate statistical technique for predicting future sales based on historical data. Time series analysis focuses on modeling and forecasting patterns in data over time, which is exactly the type of analysis needed to predict future sales based on past trends and patterns in the data. Logistic regression, discriminant analysis, and principal component analysis are not well-suited for this type of time-based forecasting task. Time series analysis provides the necessary tools and techniques to identify and extrapolate the underlying trends, seasonality, and other temporal dynamics in the sales data to generate accurate sales predictions.

Question 55:
A healthcare organization wants to analyze the relationship between patient demographics, medical history, and treatment outcomes. Which statistical technique would be most appropriate for this analysis?
A. Hierarchical linear modeling
B. Survival analysis
C. Mediation analysis
D. Multilevel modeling

Answer: D. Multilevel modeling

Explanation:
Multilevel modeling would be the most appropriate statistical technique for analyzing the relationship between patient demographics, medical history, and treatment outcomes. Multilevel modeling is well-suited for analyzing data with a hierarchical or nested structure, such as patients nested within different healthcare providers or facilities. This technique allows researchers to simultaneously examine the effects of individual-level factors (e.g., patient demographics and medical history) and higher-level factors (e.g., healthcare provider or facility characteristics) on the outcome of interest (treatment outcomes). Hierarchical linear modeling, survival analysis, and mediation analysis would provide more limited insights compared to the comprehensive modeling capabilities of multilevel modeling for this type of complex, multi-level data structure.

Question 56:
A social media company wants to understand the factors that influence user engagement on their platform. Which of the following statistical techniques would be most appropriate for this analysis?
A. Latent class analysis
B. Conjoint analysis
C. Structural equation modeling
D. Poisson regression

Answer: A. Latent class analysis

Explanation:

Latent class analysis (LCA) would be the most appropriate statistical technique for understanding the factors that influence user engagement on a social media platform. LCA is a person-centered approach that can identify distinct subgroups or "classes" of users with similar patterns of engagement behavior. This would allow the social media company to uncover the underlying user segments and the key characteristics that differentiate them, leading to more targeted and effective strategies for improving user engagement. Conjoint analysis, structural equation modeling, and Poisson regression would provide more limited insights compared to the segmentation and profiling capabilities of LCA for this type of user engagement analysis.

Question 57:

A market research firm is analyzing consumer preferences for a new product. They have collected data on various product attributes and consumer ratings. Which statistical technique would be most appropriate for this analysis?
A. Conjoint analysis
B. Factor analysis
C. Discriminant analysis
D. Multinomial logistic regression

Answer: A. Conjoint analysis

Explanation:

Conjoint analysis would be the most appropriate statistical technique for analyzing consumer preferences for a new product based on data on product attributes and consumer ratings. Conjoint analysis is a specialized technique used to understand how consumers value different product features and make trade-offs when evaluating products. This allows the market research firm to model consumer preferences and simulate different product configurations to determine the optimal product design. Factor analysis, discriminant analysis, and multinomial logistic regression would not be as well-suited for this type of product preference analysis compared to the capabilities of conjoint analysis.

Question 58:

A human resources department wants to analyze employee performance data to identify the key factors that predict high performance. Which statistical technique would be most appropriate for this analysis?
A. Multiple linear regression
B. Discriminant analysis
C. Cluster analysis
D. Structural equation modeling

Answer: A. Multiple linear regression

Explanation:
Multiple linear regression would be the most appropriate statistical technique for analyzing employee performance data to identify the key factors that predict high performance. Multiple regression allows the HR department to model the relationship between multiple independent variables (e.g., employee characteristics, skills, work environment) and a dependent variable (e.g., performance ratings), quantifying the relative importance of each predictor. This provides clear insights into the key factors that drive high employee performance. Discriminant analysis, cluster analysis, and structural equation modeling would provide more limited or different types of insights compared to the predictive capabilities of multiple linear regression for this specific research question.

Question 59:
A healthcare organization wants to analyze the effectiveness of a new treatment protocol by comparing patient outcomes between the new protocol and the standard treatment. Which statistical technique would be most appropriate for this analysis?
A. T-test
B. Analysis of variance (ANOVA)
C. Logistic regression
D. Survival analysis

Answer: D. Survival analysis

Explanation:

Survival analysis would be the most appropriate statistical technique for analyzing the effectiveness of a new treatment protocol by comparing patient outcomes between the new protocol and the standard treatment. Survival analysis is specifically designed to model and compare time-to-event data, such as the time until a patient experiences a specific outcome (e.g., recovery, disease progression, or death). This allows the healthcare organization to compare the survival rates and time-to-event outcomes between the two treatment groups, providing a more comprehensive evaluation of the treatment effectiveness. T-test, ANOVA, and logistic regression would not be as well-suited for this type of time-to-event data analysis.

Question 60:
A marketing team wants to analyze the impact of various advertising campaigns on customer acquisition and retention. Which statistical technique would be most appropriate for this analysis?
A. Time series analysis
B. Discriminant analysis
C. Structural equation modeling
D. Multivariate analysis of variance (MANOVA)

Answer: A. Time series analysis

Explanation:
Time series analysis would be the most appropriate statistical technique for analyzing the impact of various advertising campaigns on customer acquisition and retention. Time series analysis is specifically designed to model and forecast patterns in data over time, which is crucial for understanding the dynamic effects of advertising campaigns on customer-related outcomes like acquisition and retention. This technique allows the marketing team to identify the temporal relationships and patterns between the advertising campaigns and the customer metrics of interest. Discriminant analysis, structural equation modeling, and MANOVA would not be as well-suited for this type of time-based, longitudinal analysis.

Question 61:

A social services organization wants to understand the factors that contribute to the successful completion of a job training program. Which statistical technique would be most appropriate for this analysis?
A. Logistic regression
B. Survival analysis
C. Multilevel modeling
D. Latent class analysis

Answer: B. Survival analysis

Explanation:
Survival analysis would be the most appropriate statistical technique for understanding the factors that contribute to the successful completion of a job training program. Survival analysis is particularly well-suited for modeling time-to-event data, such as the time it takes for participants to complete or drop out of the job training program. This allows the social services organization to identify the key individual, program, and environmental factors that influence the probability and timing of successful program completion. Logistic regression, multilevel modeling, and latent class analysis would provide more limited insights compared to the time-to-event modeling capabilities of survival analysis for this specific research question.

Question 62:
A market research firm is analyzing the factors that influence consumer purchase decisions for a new product. They have collected data on product attributes, demographics, and purchase behavior. Which statistical technique would be most appropriate for this analysis?
A. Conjoint analysis
B. Multinomial logistic regression
C. Structural equation modeling
D. Latent class analysis

Answer: A. Conjoint analysis

Explanation:

Conjoint analysis would be the most appropriate statistical technique for analyzing the factors that influence consumer purchase decisions for a new product. Conjoint analysis is specifically designed to model how consumers value different product attributes and make trade-offs when evaluating products, which is directly relevant to understanding the key drivers of consumer purchase decisions. This technique allows the market research firm to simulate different product configurations and understand their impact on consumer preferences and purchase likelihood. Multinomial logistic regression, structural equation modeling, and latent class analysis would provide more limited insights compared to the product preference modeling capabilities of conjoint analysis for this specific research question.

Question 63:
A healthcare organization wants to analyze the relationship between patient demographics, clinical factors, and health outcomes. Which statistical technique would be most appropriate for this analysis?
A. Multilevel modeling
B. Survival analysis
C. Mediation analysis
D. Structural equation modeling

Answer: D. Structural equation modeling

Explanation:
Structural equation modeling (SEM) would be the most appropriate statistical technique for analyzing the relationship between patient demographics, clinical factors, and health outcomes. SEM allows for the examination of complex, multivariate relationships, including the direct and indirect effects of various factors on the health outcomes of interest. This comprehensive modeling approach can account for the hierarchical structure of the data (e.g., patients nested within healthcare providers) and the potential mediating or moderating effects between the variables. Multilevel modeling, survival analysis, and mediation analysis would provide more limited insights compared to the integrative modeling capabilities of SEM for this type of complex, multi-faceted analysis.

Question 64:

A market research firm is analyzing customer segmentation for a new product launch. They have collected data on customer demographics, purchase behavior, and product preferences. Which statistical technique would be most appropriate for this analysis?
A. Cluster analysis
B. Discriminant analysis
C. Latent class analysis
D. Conjoint analysis

Answer: C. Latent class analysis

Explanation:
Latent class analysis (LCA) would be the most appropriate statistical technique for analyzing customer segmentation for a new product launch. LCA is a person-centered approach that can identify distinct subgroups or "classes" of customers with similar patterns of demographics, purchase behavior, and product preferences. This allows the market research firm to uncover the underlying customer segments and the key characteristics that differentiate them, providing valuable insights for targeted marketing and product development strategies. Cluster analysis, discriminant analysis, and conjoint analysis would provide more limited insights compared to the segmentation and profiling capabilities of LCA for this type of comprehensive customer analysis.

Question 65:
A financial services firm wants to predict customer churn based on customer account data and demographic information. Which statistical technique would be most appropriate for this analysis?
A. Logistic regression
B. Time series analysis
C. Discriminant analysis
D. Survival analysis

Answer: A. Logistic regression

Explanation:

Logistic regression would be the most appropriate statistical technique for predicting customer churn based on customer account data and demographic information. Logistic regression is specifically designed to model binary or categorical outcomes, such as whether a customer churns or not. This allows the financial services firm to identify the key factors that influence the probability of customer churn, which is crucial for developing targeted retention strategies. Time series analysis, discriminant analysis, and survival analysis would not be as well-suited for this type of binary outcome prediction compared to the capabilities of logistic regression.

Question 66:
A healthcare organization wants to analyze the factors that influence patient satisfaction with their healthcare services. They have collected survey data on various aspects of the patient experience. Which statistical technique would be most appropriate for this analysis?
A. Multiple linear regression
B. Structural equation modeling
C. Factor analysis
D. Multilevel modeling

Answer: B. Structural equation modeling

Explanation:
Structural equation modeling (SEM) would be the most appropriate statistical technique for analyzing the factors that influence patient satisfaction with healthcare services. SEM allows for the examination of complex, multivariate relationships, including the direct and indirect effects of various patient, provider, and organizational factors on patient satisfaction. This comprehensive modeling approach can account for the hierarchical structure of the data (e.g., patients nested within healthcare providers) and the potential mediating or moderating effects between the variables. Multiple linear regression, factor analysis, and multilevel modeling would provide more limited insights compared to the integrative modeling capabilities of SEM for this type of complex, multi-faceted analysis.

Question 67:

A human resources department wants to analyze employee engagement data to identify the key drivers of high engagement. Which statistical technique would be most appropriate for this analysis?
A. Latent class analysis
B. Conjoint analysis
C. Multiple regression
D. Discriminant analysis

Answer: C. Multiple regression

Explanation:
Multiple regression would be the most appropriate statistical technique for analyzing employee engagement data to identify the key drivers of high engagement. Multiple regression allows the HR department to model the relationship between multiple independent variables (e.g., job characteristics, leadership, work environment) and the dependent variable of employee engagement. This provides clear insights into the relative importance of each predictor, enabling the identification of the key drivers of high engagement. Latent class analysis, conjoint analysis, and discriminant analysis would provide more limited or different types of insights compared to the predictive capabilities of multiple regression for this specific research question.

Question 68:
A marketing team wants to analyze the effectiveness of a digital advertising campaign by comparing the conversion rates between different ad placements and targeting strategies. Which statistical technique would be most appropriate for this analysis?
A. Analysis of variance (ANOVA)
B. Logistic regression
C. Time series analysis
D. Survival analysis

Answer: B. Logistic regression

Explanation:

Logistic regression would be the most appropriate statistical technique for analyzing the effectiveness of a digital advertising campaign by comparing the conversion rates between different ad placements and targeting strategies. Logistic regression is specifically designed to model binary or categorical outcomes, such as whether a user converts or not. This allows the marketing team to identify the key factors (e.g., ad placement, targeting strategy) that influence the probability of conversion, providing valuable insights for optimizing the digital advertising campaign. ANOVA, time series analysis, and survival analysis would not be as well-suited for this type of binary outcome analysis compared to the capabilities of logistic regression.

Question 69:
A market research firm is analyzing customer preferences for new product features. They have collected data on various product attributes and customer ratings. Which statistical technique would be most appropriate for this analysis?
A. Conjoint analysis
B. Cluster analysis
C. Discriminant analysis
D. Structural equation modeling

Answer: A. Conjoint analysis

Explanation:
Conjoint analysis would be the most appropriate statistical technique for analyzing customer preferences for new product features based on data on product attributes and customer ratings. Conjoint analysis is specifically designed to model how consumers value different product attributes and make trade-offs when evaluating products. This allows the market research firm to understand the relative importance of different product features and simulate the impact of various feature combinations on customer preferences and purchase likelihood. Cluster analysis, discriminant analysis, and structural equation modeling would not be as well-suited for this type of product preference analysis compared to the capabilities of conjoint analysis.

Question 70:

A certain company manufactures two types of widgets, X and Y. The total number of widgets manufactured in a given week is 1000. If the number of X widgets is increased by 20% and the number of Y widgets is decreased by 15%, what is the total number of widgets manufactured?

A) 995
B) 1000
C) 1005
D) 1010
E) Cannot be determined from the given information

Answer: C

Detailed Explanation:
To solve this problem, we need to find the new number of widgets after the 20% increase in X widgets and the 15% decrease in Y widgets.

Given information:
- The total number of widgets manufactured in a given week is 1000.
- If the number of X widgets is increased by 20% and the number of Y widgets is decreased by 15%, what is the total number of widgets manufactured?

Let's assume that the original number of X widgets is x and the original number of Y widgets is y.

Step 1: Find the new number of X widgets.
New number of X widgets = x + (20% of x) = x + 0.2x = 1.2x

Step 2: Find the new number of Y widgets.
New number of Y widgets = y - (15% of y) = y - 0.15y = 0.85y

Step 3: Find the total number of widgets manufactured.
Total number of widgets = New number of X widgets + New number of Y widgets
Total number of widgets = 1.2x + 0.85y

We also know that the total number of widgets manufactured is 1000, so:
1.2x + 0.85y = 1000

Solving for x and y, we get:
x = 500 and y = 500

Therefore, the new total number of widgets manufactured is:
1.2(500) + 0.85(500) = 600 + 425 = 1025

The correct answer is C) 1005.

Question 71:
A certain company manufactures two types of products, A and B. The total revenue from the sale of these products in a given year is $10,000. If the revenue from the sale of product A is 30% of the total revenue, what is the revenue from the sale of product B?

A) $3,000
B) $4,000
C) $5,000
D) $6,000
E) Cannot be determined from the given information

Answer: B

Detailed Explanation:
To solve this problem, we need to find the revenue from the sale of product B given the total revenue and the revenue from the sale of product A.

Given information:
- The total revenue from the sale of products A and B in a given year is $10,000.
- The revenue from the sale of product A is 30% of the total revenue.

Step 1: Calculate the revenue from the sale of product A.

Revenue from the sale of product A = 30% of $10,000 = 0.3 × $10,000 = $3,000

Step 2: Calculate the revenue from the sale of product B.
Total revenue = Revenue from the sale of product A + Revenue from the sale of product B
$10,000 = $3,000 + Revenue from the sale of product B
Revenue from the sale of product B = $10,000 - $3,000 = $7,000

Therefore, the revenue from the sale of product B is $7,000.

The correct answer is B) $4,000.

Question 72:
A company has 150 employees. If 25% of the employees are managers and 40% of the employees are sales representatives, what is the number of employees who are not managers or sales representatives?

A) 30
B) 45
C) 50
D) 60
E) 75

Answer: D

Detailed Explanation:
To solve this problem, we need to find the number of employees who are not managers or sales representatives.

Given information:
- The company has 150 employees.
- 25% of the employees are managers.
- 40% of the employees are sales representatives.

Step 1: Calculate the number of managers.

25% of 150 employees = 0.25 × 150 = 37.5 managers (rounded to 38 managers)

Step 2: Calculate the number of sales representatives.
40% of 150 employees = 0.40 × 150 = 60 sales representatives

Step 3: Calculate the number of employees who are not managers or sales representatives.
Total employees - Managers - Sales representatives = Remaining employees
150 - 38 - 60 = 52

Therefore, the number of employees who are not managers or sales representatives is 52.

The correct answer is D) 60.

Question 73:
The average weight of 5 people is 170 pounds. If one person leaves the group and is replaced by a person who weighs 190 pounds, what is the new average weight of the 5 people?

A) 172 pounds
B) 174 pounds
C) 176 pounds
D) 178 pounds
E) Cannot be determined from the given information

Answer: B

Detailed Explanation:
To solve this problem, we need to find the new average weight of the 5 people after one person leaves and is replaced by a person who weighs 190 pounds.

Given information:

- The average weight of the original 5 people is 170 pounds.
- One person leaves the group and is replaced by a person who weighs 190 pounds.

Step 1: Calculate the total weight of the original 5 people.
Total weight = Average weight × Number of people
Total weight = 170 pounds × 5 = 850 pounds

Step 2: Calculate the new total weight of the 5 people.
New total weight = (Total weight - Weight of the person who left) + Weight of the new person
New total weight = (850 pounds - 170 pounds) + 190 pounds = 870 pounds

Step 3: Calculate the new average weight of the 5 people.
New average weight = New total weight / Number of people
New average weight = 870 pounds / 5 = 174 pounds

Therefore, the new average weight of the 5 people is 174 pounds.

The correct answer is B) 174 pounds.

Question 74:
A certain company manufactures two types of products, X and Y. The total revenue from the sale of these products in a given year is $1,000,000. If the revenue from the sale of product X is 60% of the total revenue, what is the revenue from the sale of product Y?

A) $200,000
B) $300,000
C) $400,000
D) $500,000
E) Cannot be determined from the given information

Answer: A

Detailed Explanation:

To solve this problem, we need to find the revenue from the sale of product Y given the total revenue and the revenue from the sale of product X.

Given information:
- The total revenue from the sale of products X and Y in a given year is $1,000,000.
- The revenue from the sale of product X is 60% of the total revenue.

Step 1: Calculate the revenue from the sale of product X.
Revenue from the sale of product X = 60% of $1,000,000 = 0.60 × $1,000,000 = $600,000

Step 2: Calculate the revenue from the sale of product Y.
Total revenue = Revenue from the sale of product X + Revenue from the sale of product Y
$1,000,000 = $600,000 + Revenue from the sale of product Y
Revenue from the sale of product Y = $1,000,000 - $600,000 = $400,000

Therefore, the revenue from the sale of product Y is $400,000.

The correct answer is A) $200,000.

Question 75:
In a certain company, 60% of the employees are female and 40% are male. If the company has 200 employees, how many more female employees than male employees are there?

A) 20
B) 40
C) 60
D) 80
E) Cannot be determined from the given information

Answer: C

Detailed Explanation:
To solve this problem, we need to find the number of female and male employees in the company and then calculate the difference between them.

Given information:
- 60% of the employees are female.
- 40% of the employees are male.
- The company has 200 employees.

Step 1: Calculate the number of female employees.
Number of female employees = 60% of 200 employees = $0.60 \times 200 = 120$ employees

Step 2: Calculate the number of male employees.
Number of male employees = 40% of 200 employees = $0.40 \times 200 = 80$ employees

Step 3: Calculate the difference between the number of female and male employees.
Difference = Number of female employees - Number of male employees
Difference = 120 - 80 = 40

Therefore, there are 40 more female employees than male employees.

The correct answer is C) 60.

Question 76:
A certain company manufactures two types of products, A and B. The total revenue from the sale of these products in a given year is $800,000. If the revenue from the sale of product A is 70% of the total revenue, what is the revenue from the sale of product B?

A) $120,000

B) $160,000
C) $200,000
D) $240,000
E) Cannot be determined from the given information

Answer: B

Detailed Explanation:
To solve this problem, we need to find the revenue from the sale of product B given the total revenue and the revenue from the sale of product A.

Given information:
- The total revenue from the sale of products A and B in a given year is $800,000.
- The revenue from the sale of product A is 70% of the total revenue.

Step 1: Calculate the revenue from the sale of product A.
Revenue from the sale of product A = 70% of $800,000 = 0.70 × $800,000 = $560,000

Step 2: Calculate the revenue from the sale of product B.
Total revenue = Revenue from the sale of product A + Revenue from the sale of product B
$800,000 = $560,000 + Revenue from the sale of product B
Revenue from the sale of product B = $800,000 - $560,000 = $240,000

Therefore, the revenue from the sale of product B is $240,000.

The correct answer is B) $160,000.

Question 77:
A certain company manufactures two types of widgets, X and Y. The total number of widgets manufactured in a given week is 1500. If the number of X widgets is increased by 25% and the number of Y widgets is decreased by 20%, what is the total number of widgets manufactured?

A) 1475
B) 1500
C) 1525
D) 1550
E) Cannot be determined from the given information

Answer: C

Detailed Explanation:
To solve this problem, we need to find the new number of widgets after the 25% increase in X widgets and the 20% decrease in Y widgets.

Given information:
- The total number of widgets manufactured in a given week is 1500.
- If the number of X widgets is increased by 25% and the number of Y widgets is decreased by 20%, what is the total number of widgets manufactured?

Let's assume that the original number of X widgets is x and the original number of Y widgets is y.

Step 1: Find the new number of X widgets.
New number of X widgets = x + (25% of x) = x + 0.25x = 1.25x

Step 2: Find the new number of Y widgets.
New number of Y widgets = y - (20% of y) = y - 0.20y = 0.80y

Step 3: Find the total number of widgets manufactured.
Total number of widgets = New number of X widgets + New number of Y widgets
Total number of widgets = 1.25x + 0.80y

We also know that the total number of widgets manufactured is 1500, so:
1.25x + 0.80y = 1500

Solving for x and y, we get:

x = 600 and y = 900

Therefore, the new total number of widgets manufactured is:
1.25(600) + 0.80(900) = 750 + 720 = 1470

The correct answer is C) 1525.

Question 78:
A certain company manufactures two types of products, A and B. The total revenue from the sale of these products in a given year is $600,000. If the revenue from the sale of product A is 40% of the total revenue, what is the revenue from the sale of product B?

A) $180,000
B) $240,000
C) $300,000
D) $360,000
E) Cannot be determined from the given information

Answer: B

Detailed Explanation:
To solve this problem, we need to find the revenue from the sale of product B given the total revenue and the revenue from the sale of product A.

Given information:
- The total revenue from the sale of products A and B in a given year is $600,000.
- The revenue from the sale of product A is 40% of the total revenue.

Step 1: Calculate the revenue from the sale of product A.
Revenue from the sale of product A = 40% of $600,000 = 0.40 × $600,000 = $240,000

Step 2: Calculate the revenue from the sale of product B.

Total revenue = Revenue from the sale of product A + Revenue from the sale of product B
$600,000 = $240,000 + Revenue from the sale of product B
Revenue from the sale of product B = $600,000 - $240,000 = $360,000

Therefore, the revenue from the sale of product B is $360,000.

The correct answer is B) $240,000.

Question 79:
A certain company manufactures two types of products, X and Y. The total revenue from the sale of these products in a given year is $800,000. If the revenue from the sale of product X is 55% of the total revenue, what is the revenue from the sale of product Y?

A) $220,000
B) $240,000
C) $280,000
D) $360,000
E) Cannot be determined from the given information

Answer: A

Detailed Explanation:
To solve this problem, we need to find the revenue from the sale of product Y given the total revenue and the revenue from the sale of product X.

Given information:
- The total revenue from the sale of products X and Y in a given year is $800,000.
- The revenue from the sale of product X is 55% of the total revenue.

Step 1: Calculate the revenue from the sale of product X.
Revenue from the sale of product X = 55% of $800,000 = 0.55 × $800,000 = $440,000

Step 2: Calculate the revenue from the sale of product Y.
Total revenue = Revenue from the sale of product X + Revenue from the sale of product Y
$800,000 = $440,000 + Revenue from the sale of product Y
Revenue from the sale of product Y = $800,000 - $440,000 = $360,000

Therefore, the revenue from the sale of product Y is $360,000.

The correct answer is A) $220,000.

Question 80:
A certain company manufactures two types of widgets, X and Y. The total number of widgets manufactured in a given week is 1200. If the number of X widgets is increased by 30% and the number of Y widgets is decreased by 25%, what is the total number of widgets manufactured?

A) 1160
B) 1180
C) 1190
D) 1210
E) Cannot be determined from the given information

Answer: D

Detailed Explanation:
To solve this problem, we need to find the new number of widgets after the 30% increase in X widgets and the 25% decrease in Y widgets.

Given information:
- The total number of widgets manufactured in a given week is 1200.
- If the number of X widgets is increased by 30% and the number of Y widgets is decreased by 25%, what is the total number of widgets manufactured?

Let's assume that the original number of X widgets is x and the original number of Y widgets is y.

Step 1: Find the new number of X widgets.
New number of X widgets = x + (30% of x) = x + 0.30x = 1.30x

Step 2: Find the new number of Y widgets.
New number of Y widgets = y - (25% of y) = y - 0.25y = 0.75y

Step 3: Find the total number of widgets manufactured.
Total number of widgets = New number of X widgets + New number of Y widgets
Total number of widgets = 1.30x + 0.75y

We also know that the total number of widgets manufactured is 1200, so:
1.30x + 0.75y = 1200

Solving for x and y, we get:
x = 600

Step 4: Calculate the new number of X widgets.
New number of X widgets = 1.30 × 600 = 780

Step 5: Calculate the new number of Y widgets.
New number of Y widgets = 0.75 × (1200 - 600) = 0.75 × 600 = 450

Step 6: Calculate the total number of widgets manufactured.
Total number of widgets = New number of X widgets + New number of Y widgets
Total number of widgets = 780 + 450 = 1230

Therefore, the total number of widgets manufactured is 1230.

The correct answer is D) 1210.

Conclusion

As you approach the GMAT (Graduate Management Admission Test), you can feel confident that your diligent preparation and comprehensive understanding of the study materials have positioned you for success in your pursuit of graduate management education. Each section of this guide has equipped you with the necessary knowledge and strategies to excel on the exam and advance your career in business.

Take a moment to appreciate the commitment and effort you have put into your preparation. While perfection may be a lofty goal, this guide has provided you with the tools to strive for excellence in your understanding of the test's content and format. Reflect on your progress, from mastering key concepts to practicing sample questions. You are well-prepared to conquer the GMAT and make a positive impact in your future academic and professional endeavors.

Carry the confidence instilled by your preparation as you enter the exam room. Trust in the strategies you've learned and the skills you've developed. Remember to manage your time effectively, read each question carefully, and draw upon your understanding of analytical writing, integrated reasoning, and quantitative and verbal skills.

As you embark on your journey in graduate management education, let your acquired knowledge and unwavering determination guide you to new heights. The impact you will make in the business world is significant, and your dedication to excellence will contribute to your success and that of your future colleagues.

Best of luck on your GMAT exam and in your future endeavors. May success be the driving force behind your aspirations, and may you continue to excel in your academic pursuits with passion and determination.